DINOSAUR
Coloring Book
For Kids

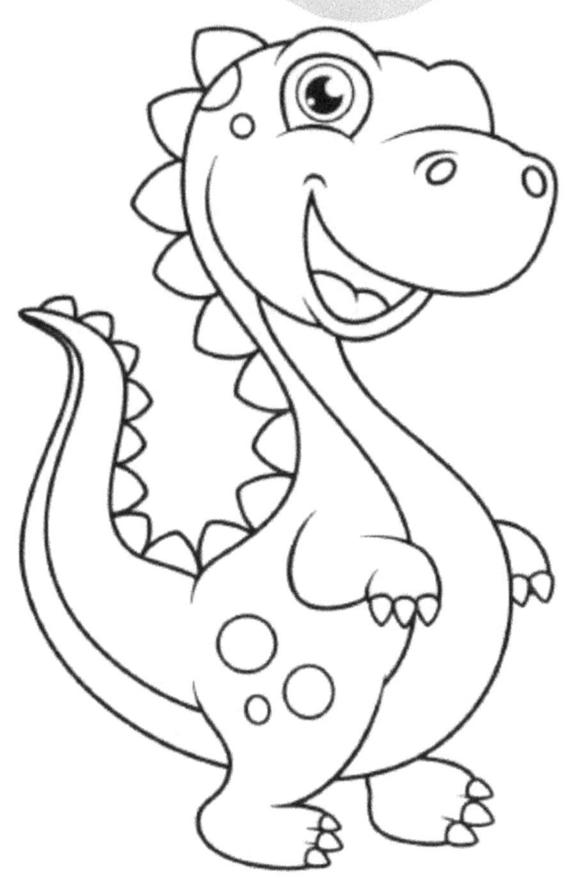

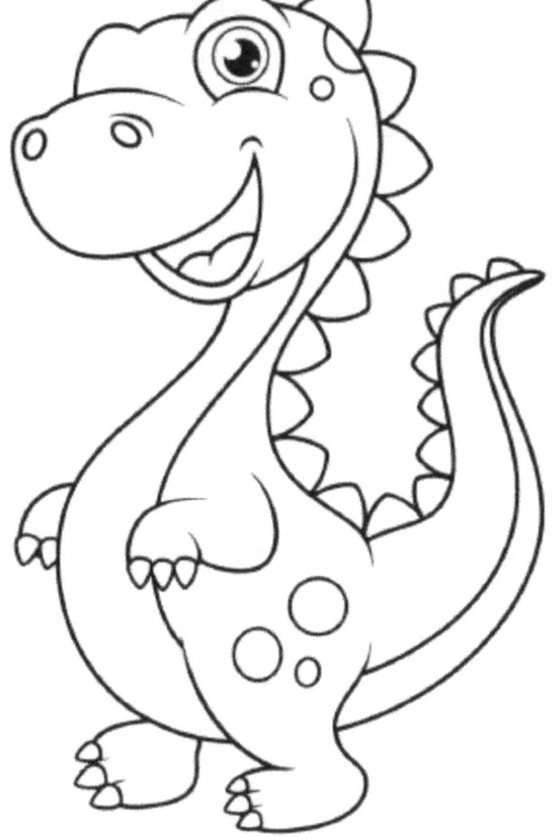

THIS BOOK BELONG TO

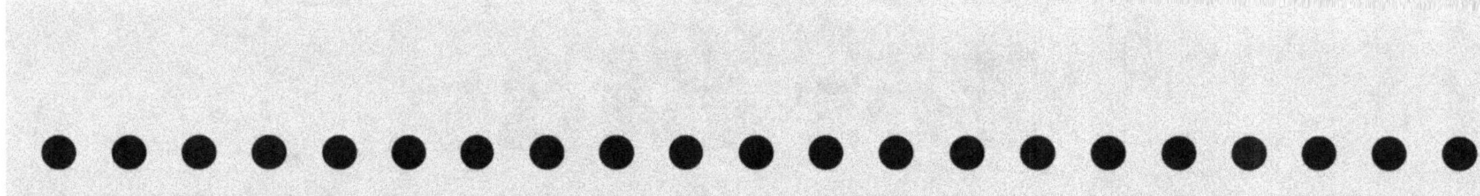

· ·

· ·

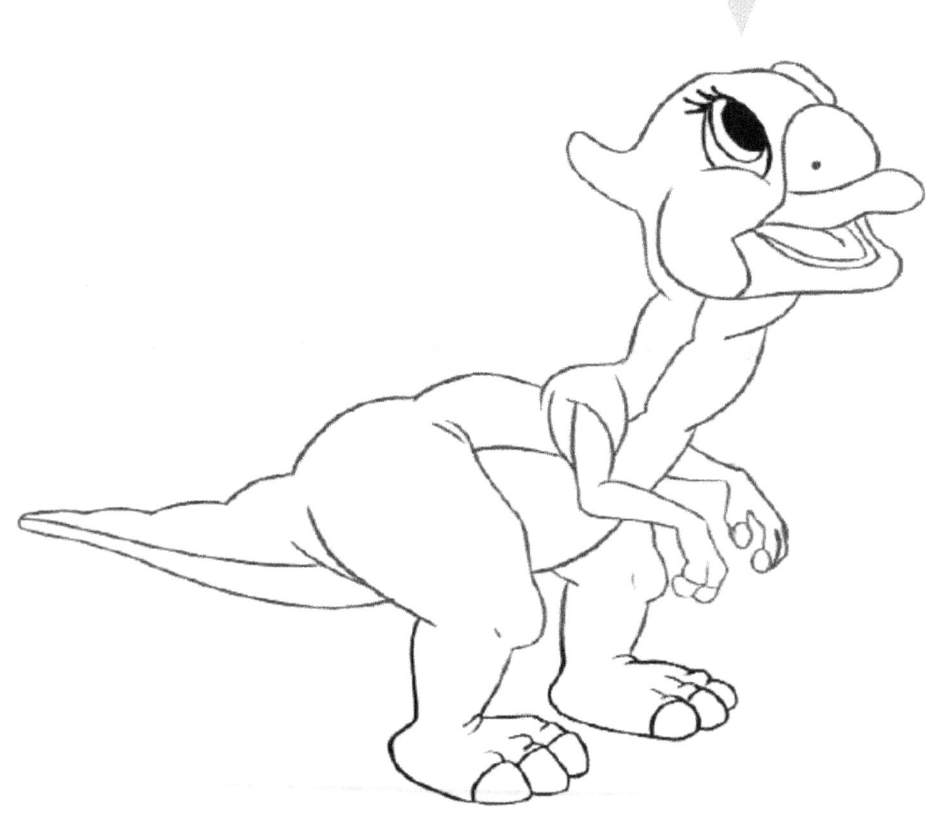

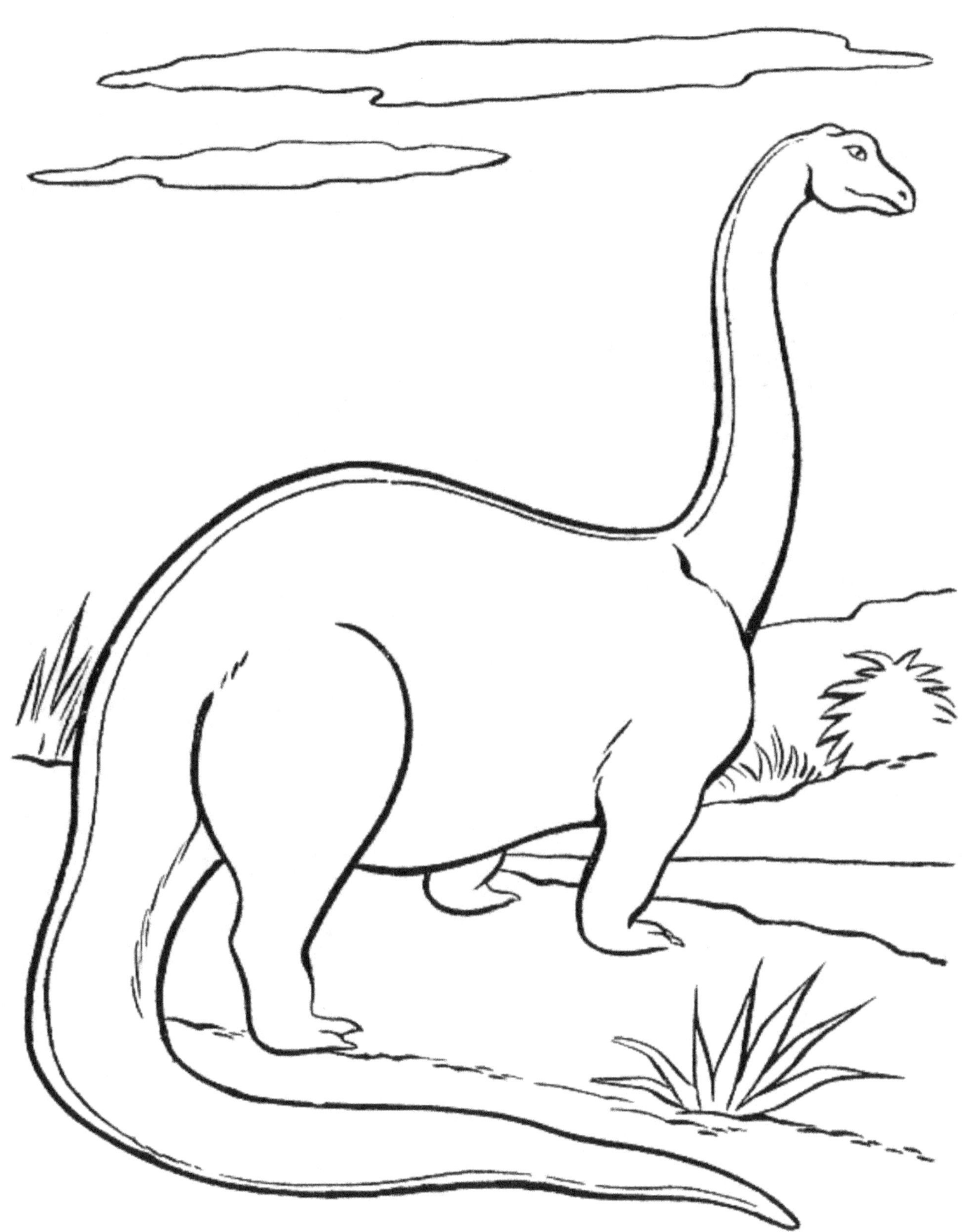

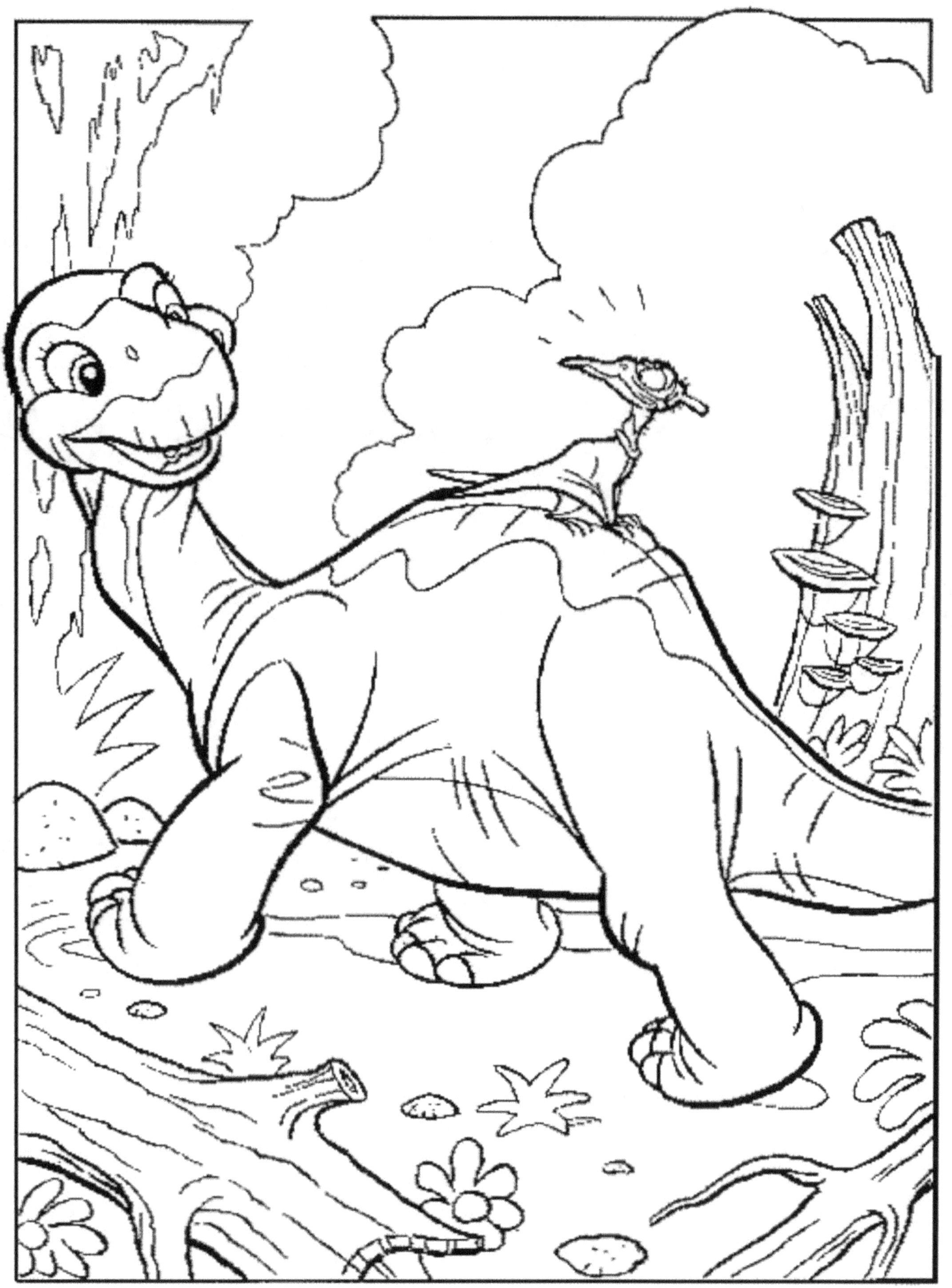

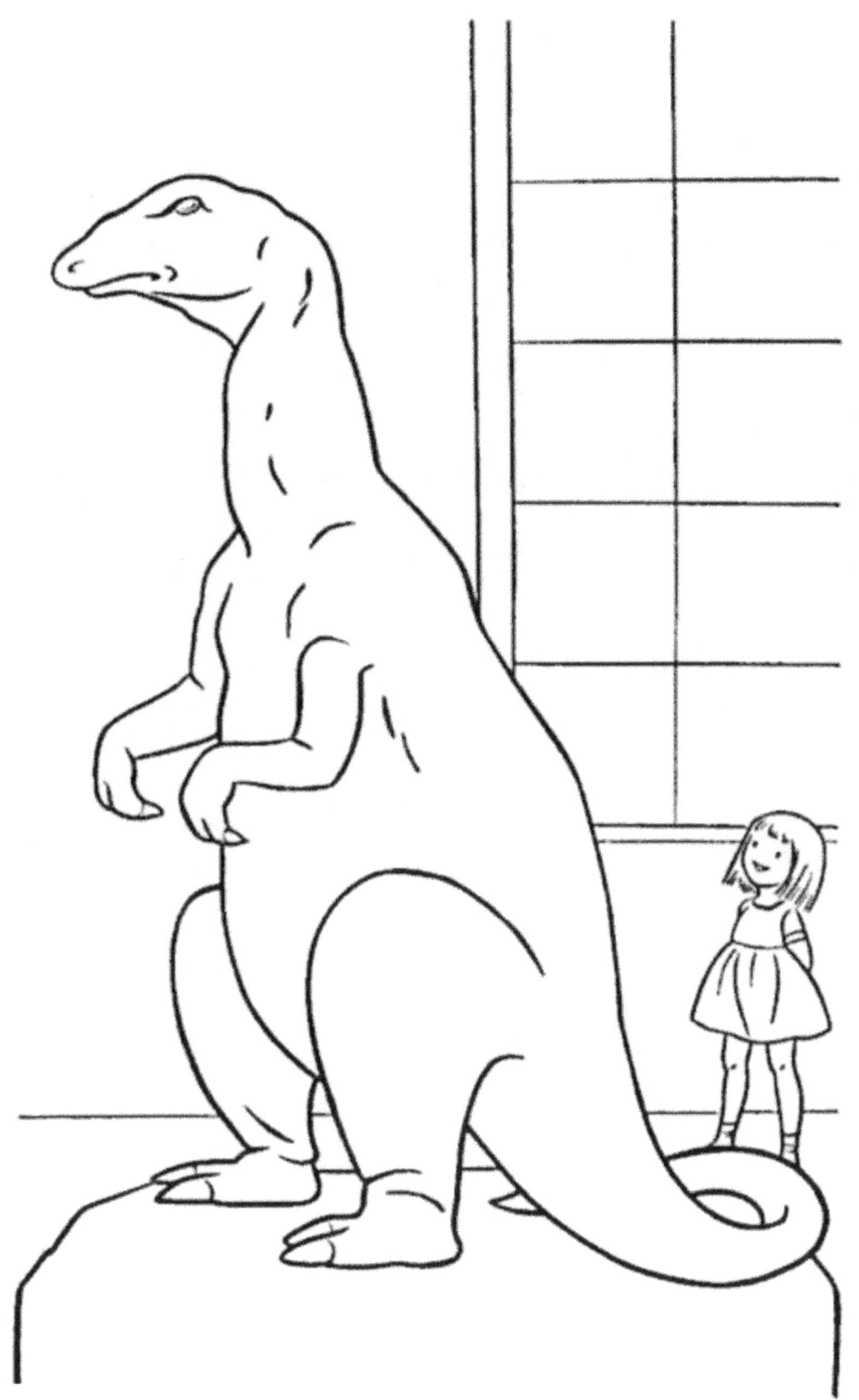

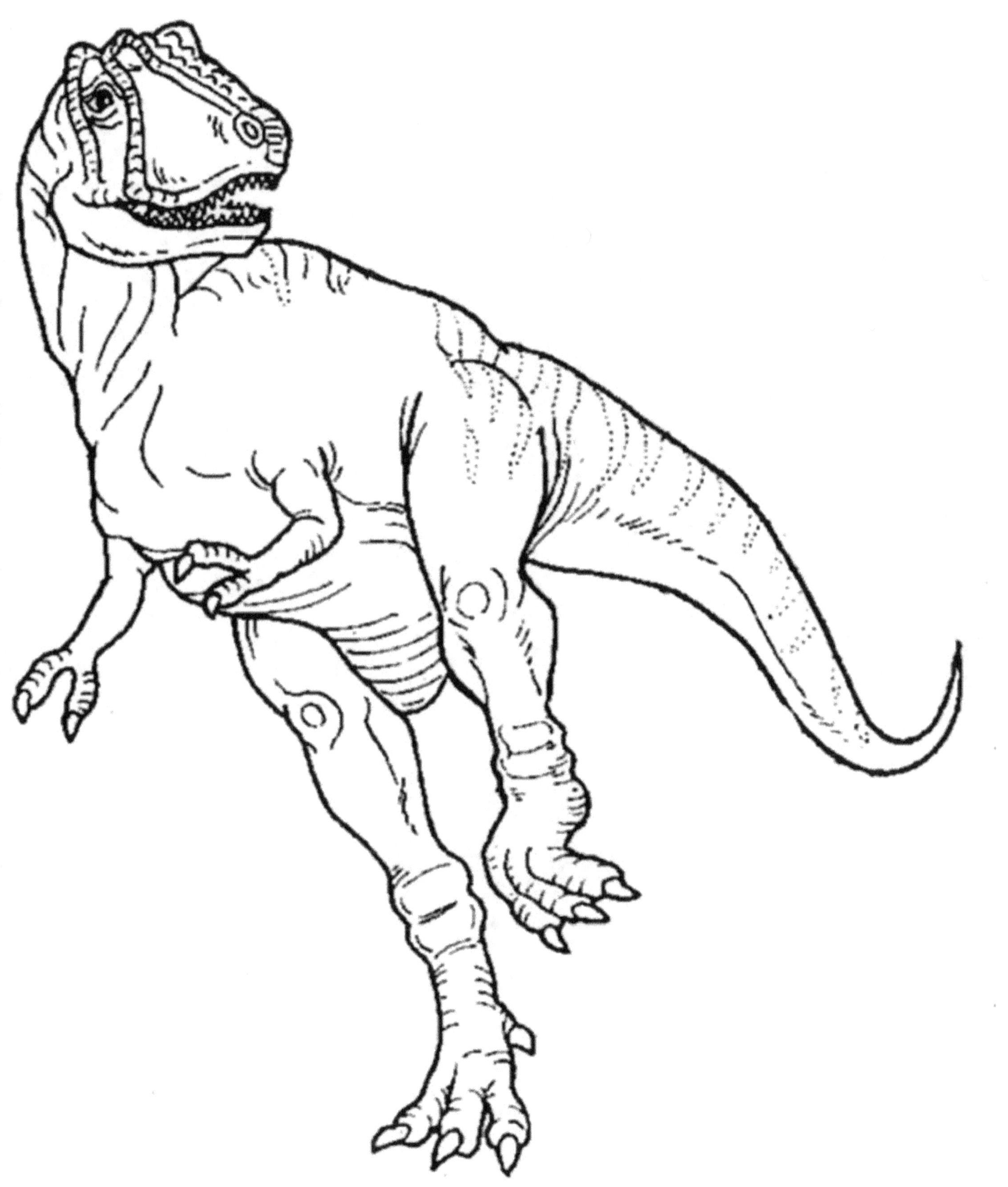

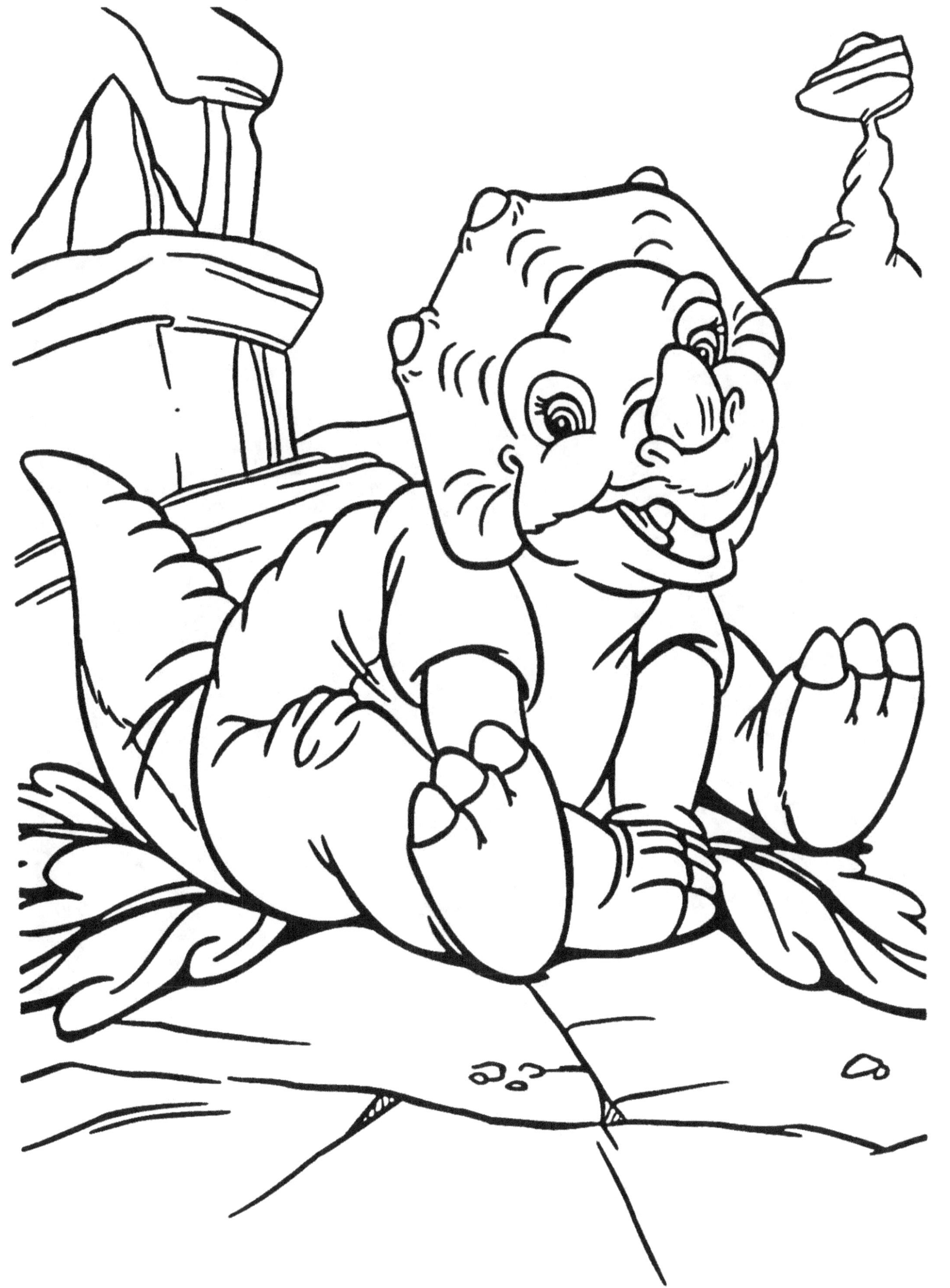

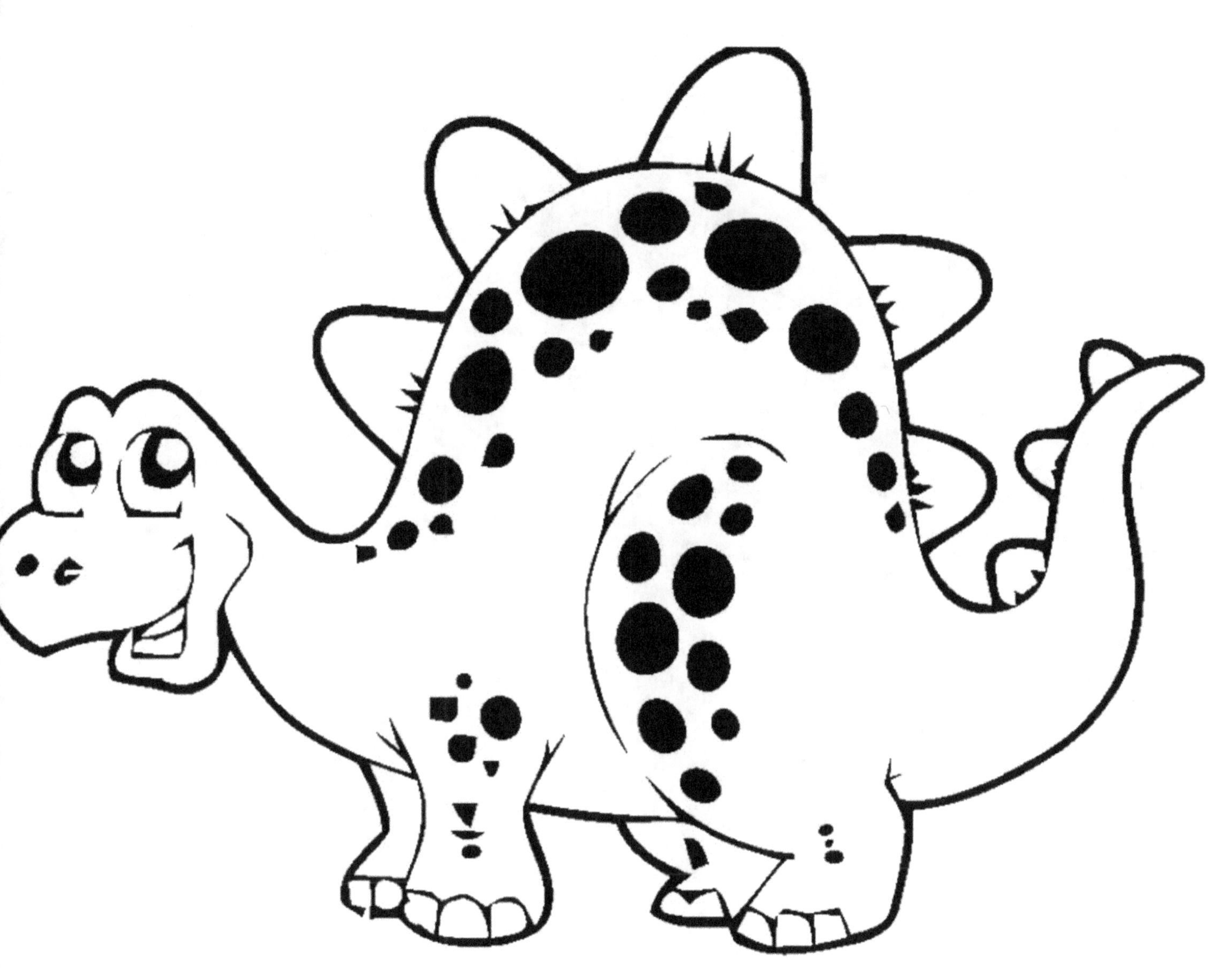

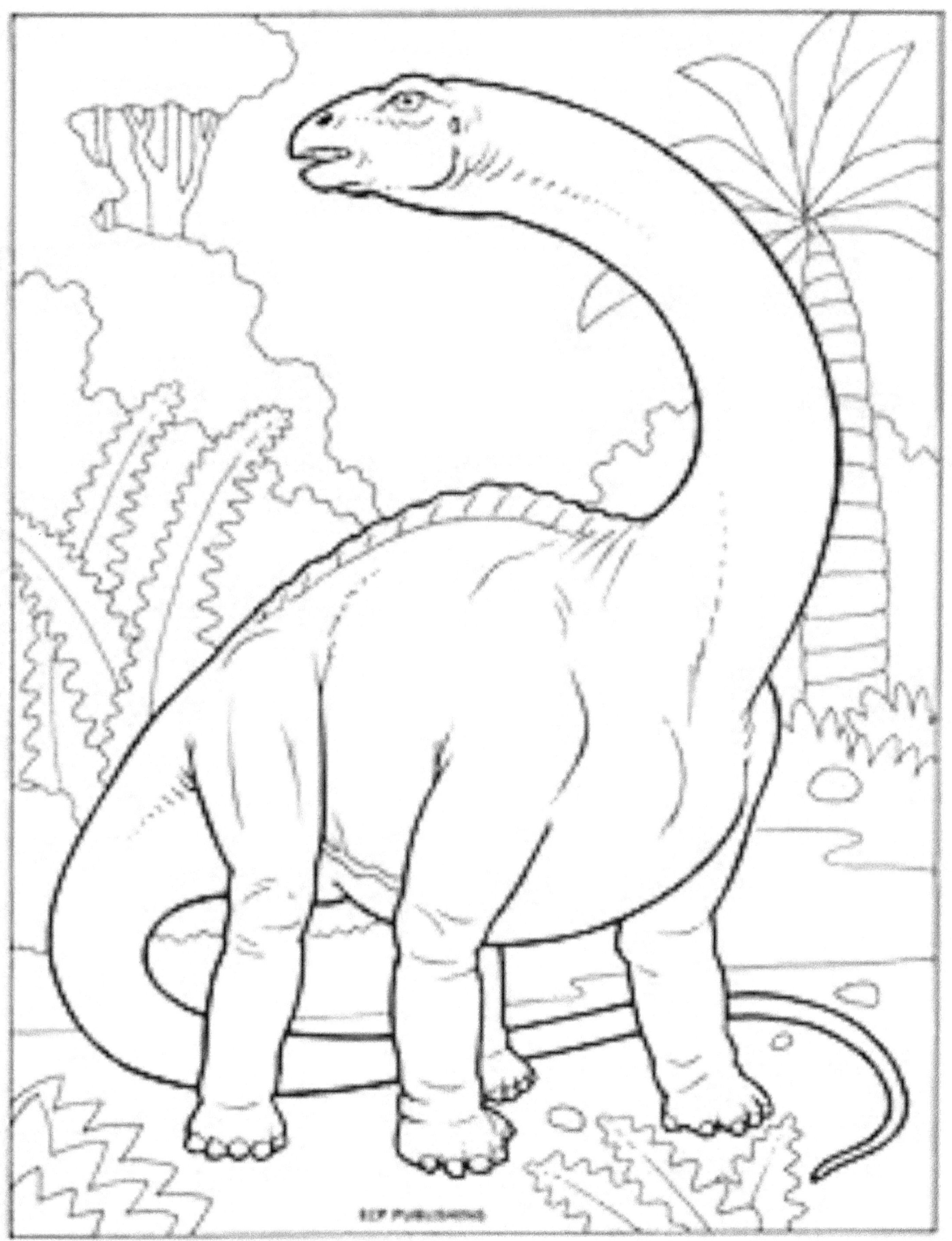

ELF PUBLISHING

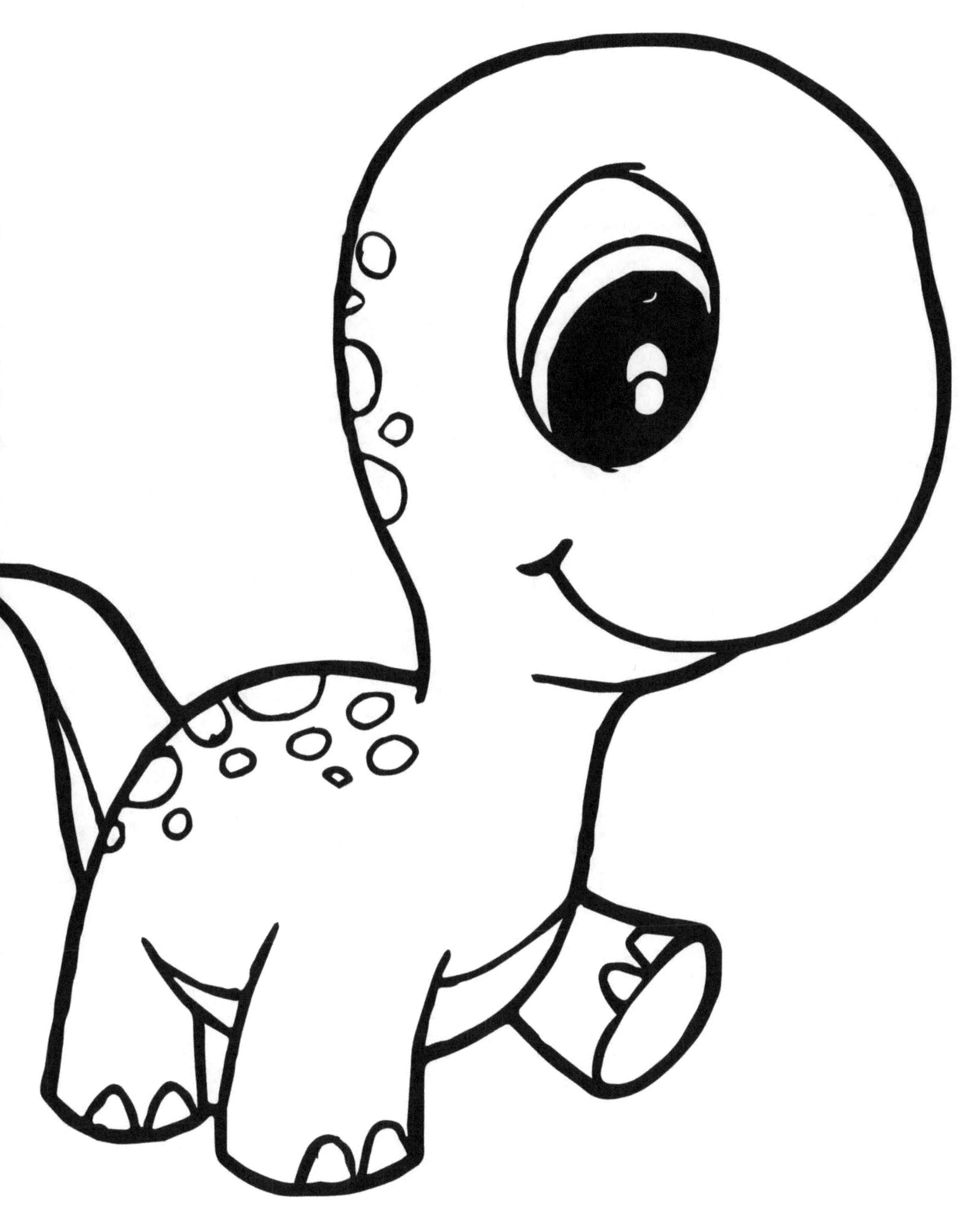

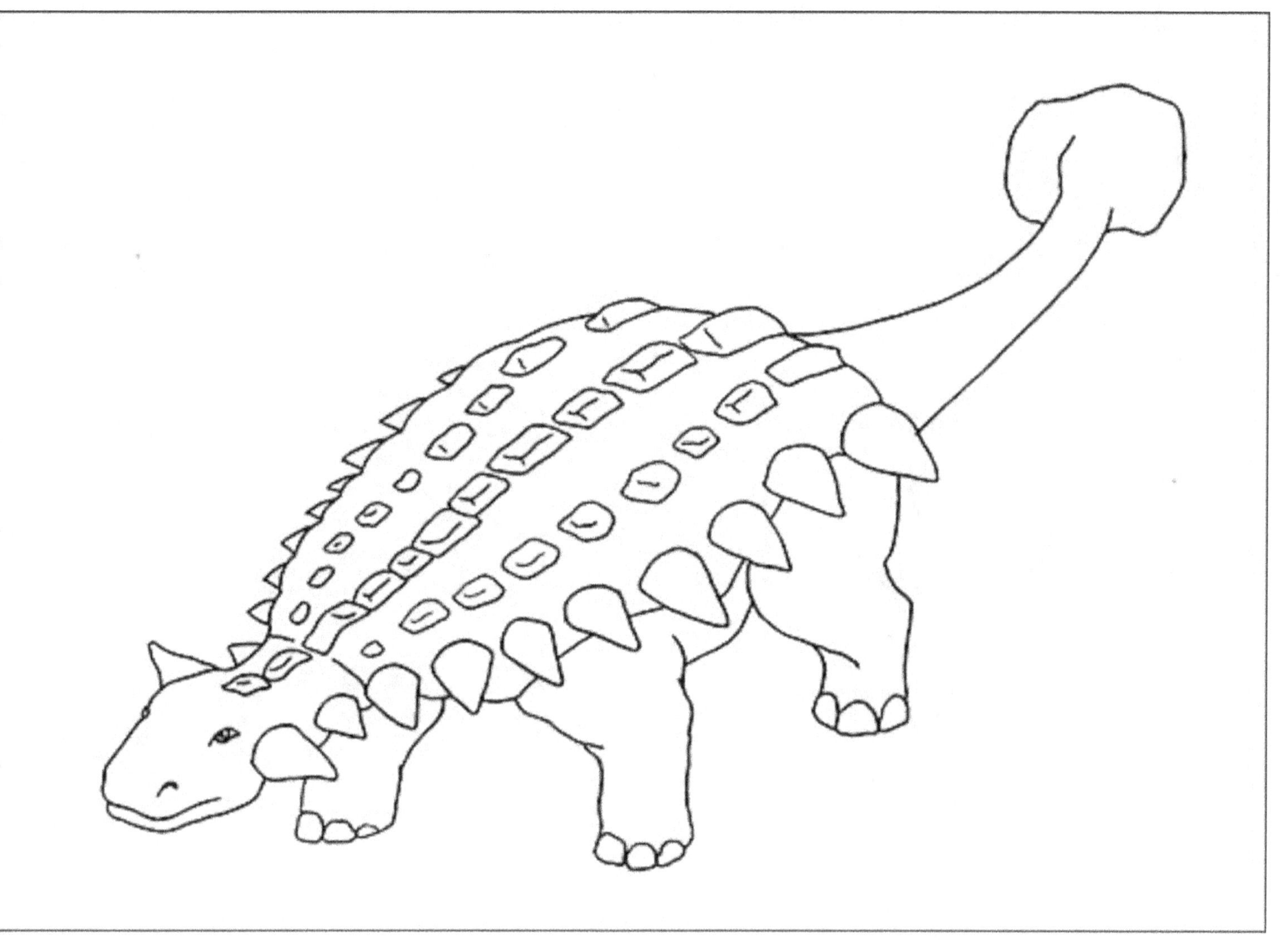

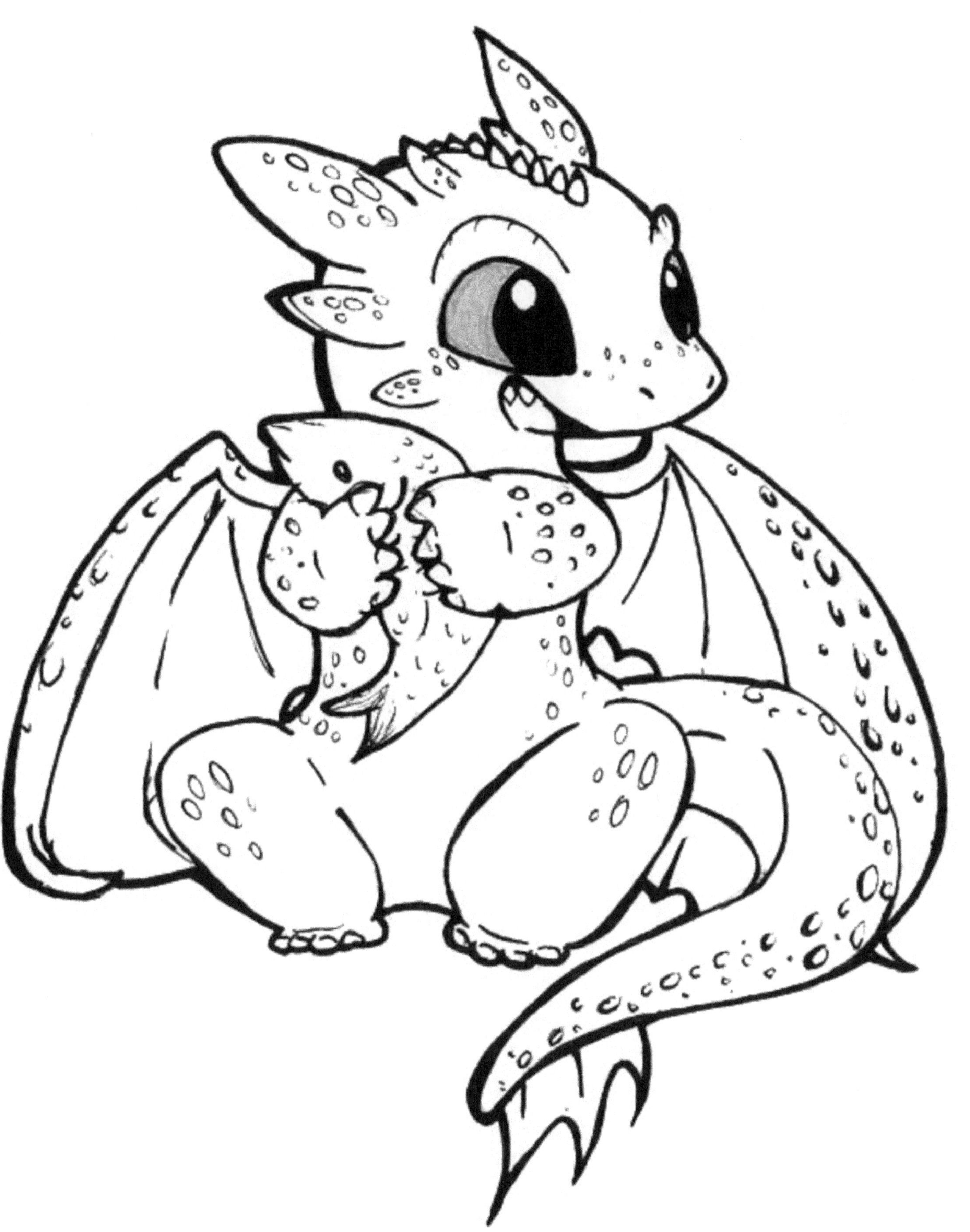

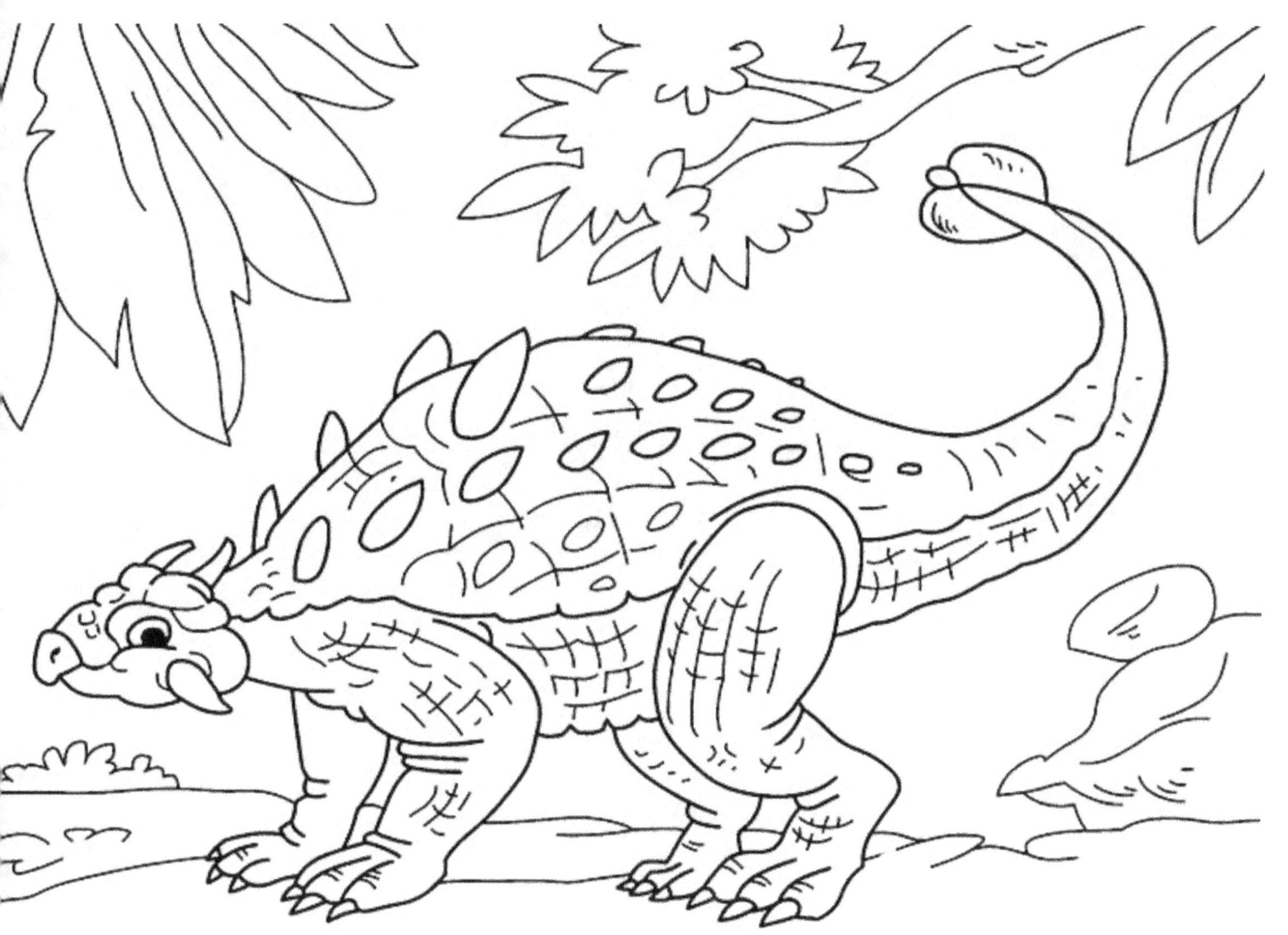

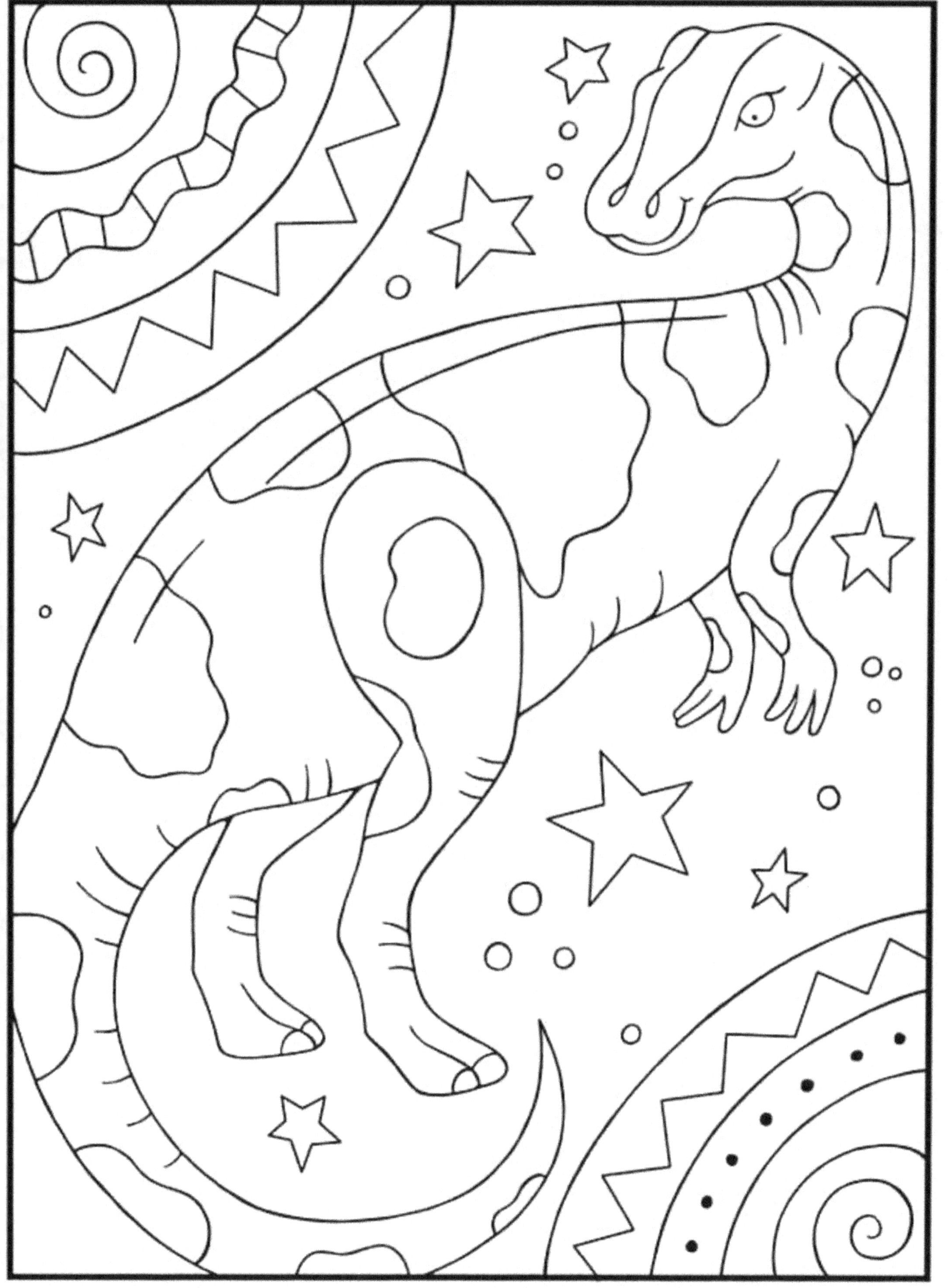

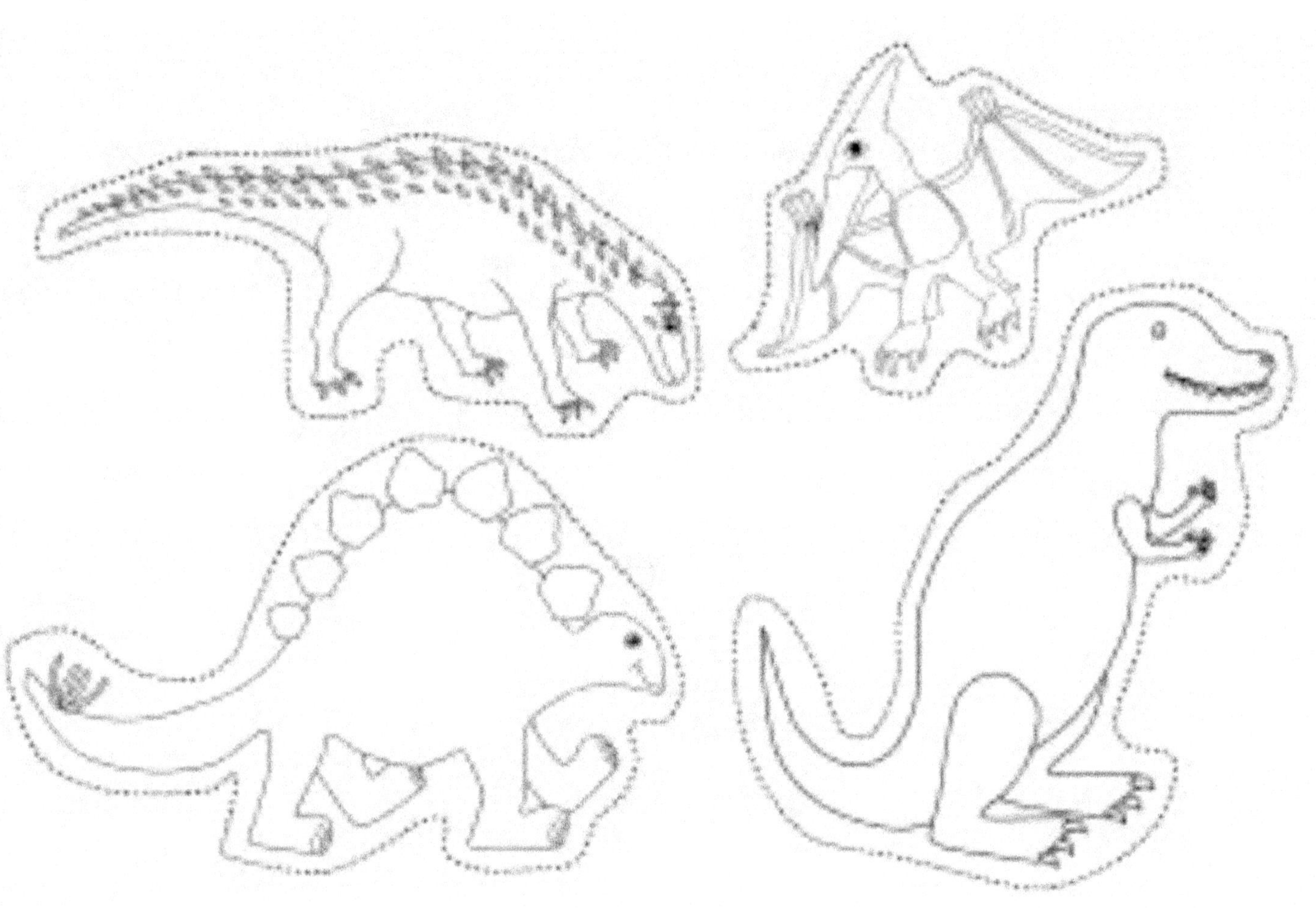

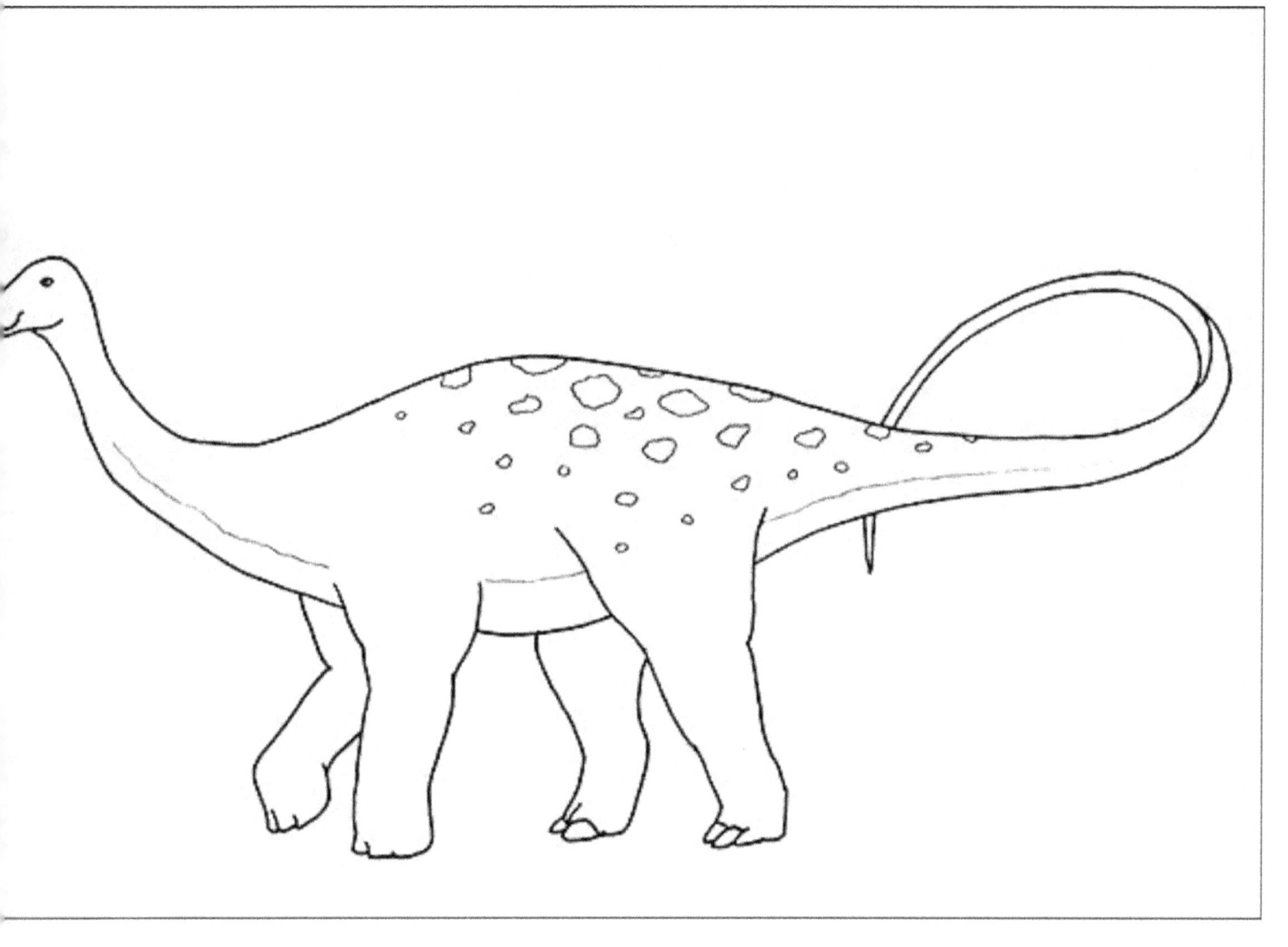

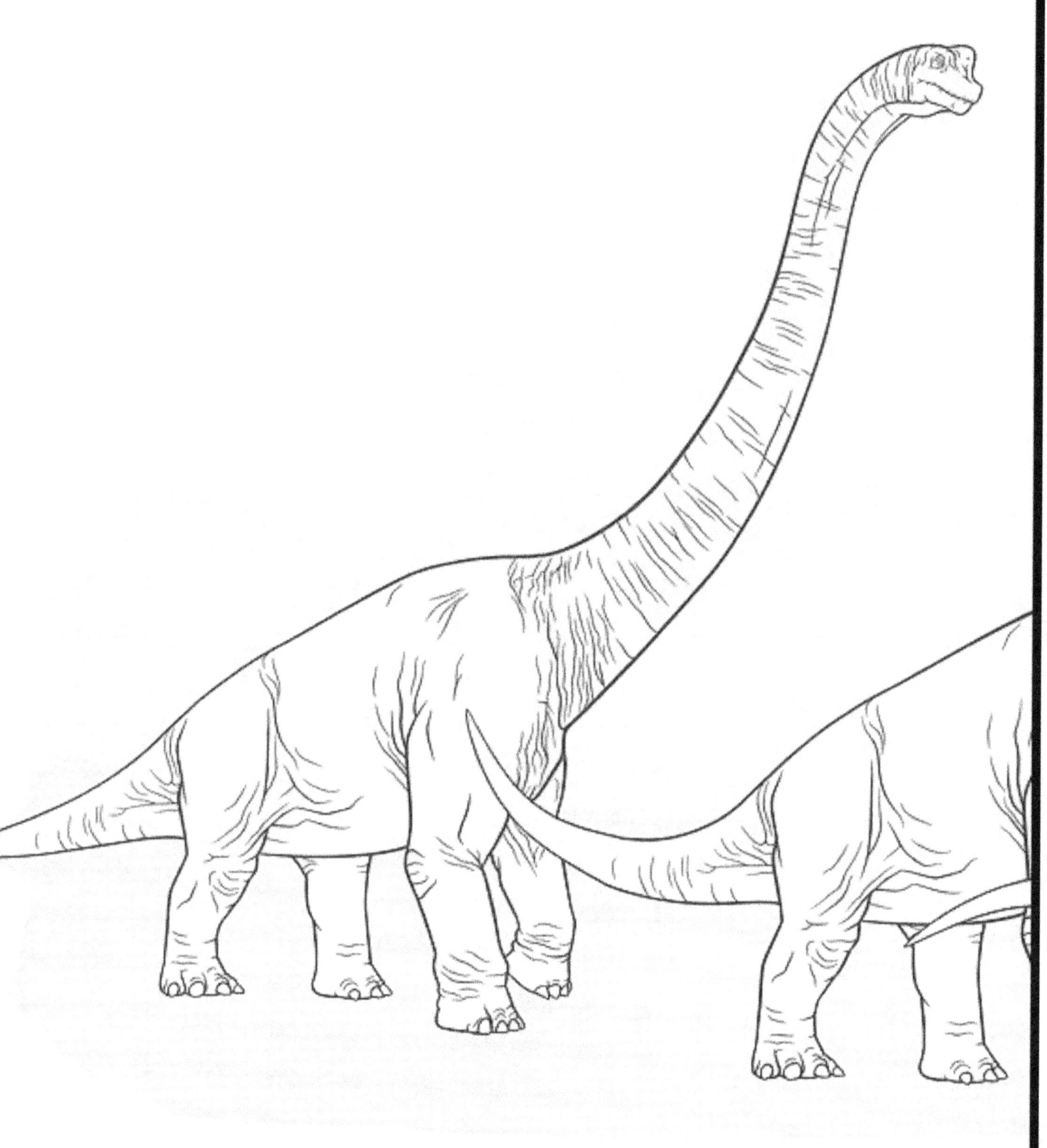

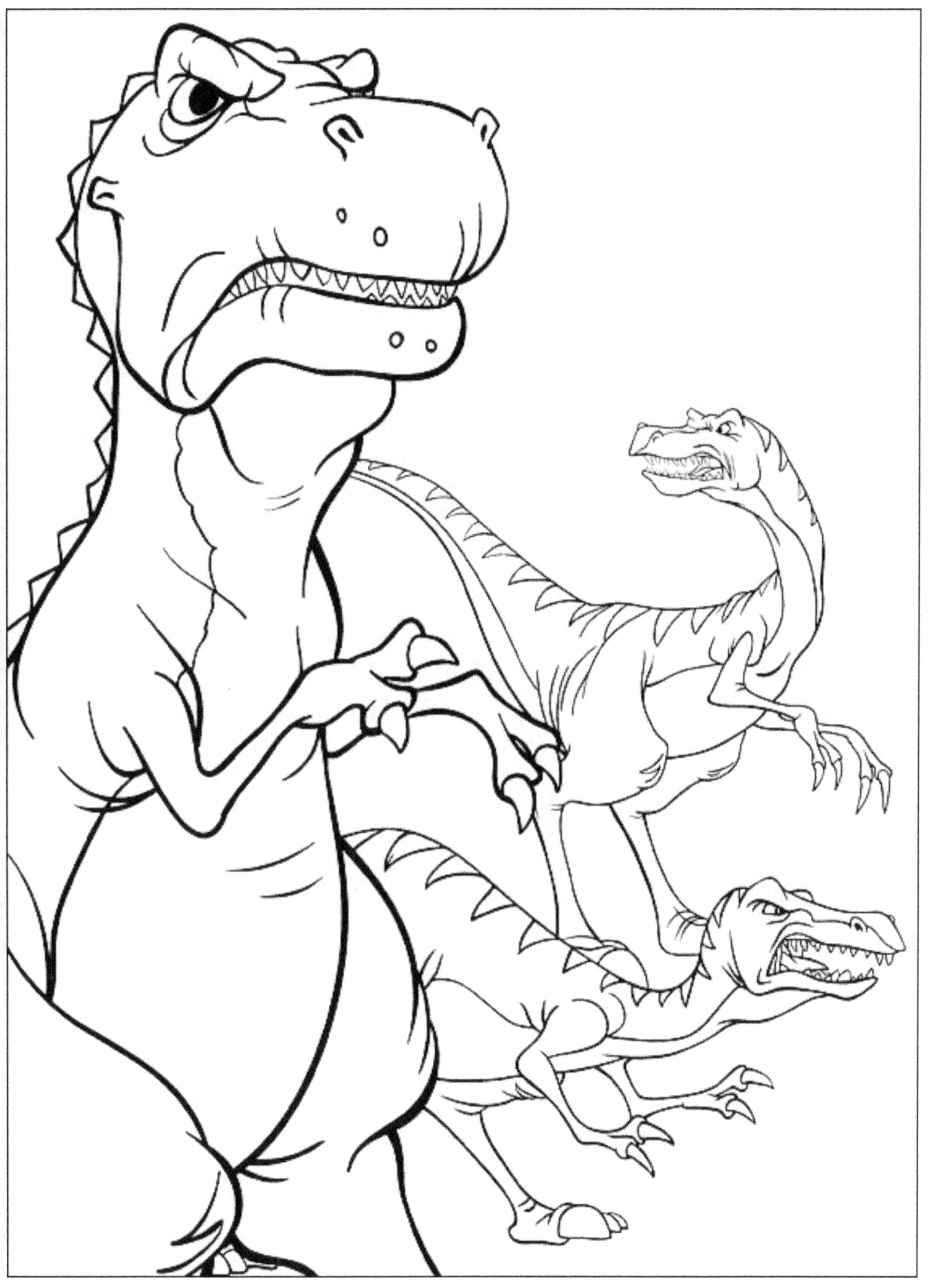

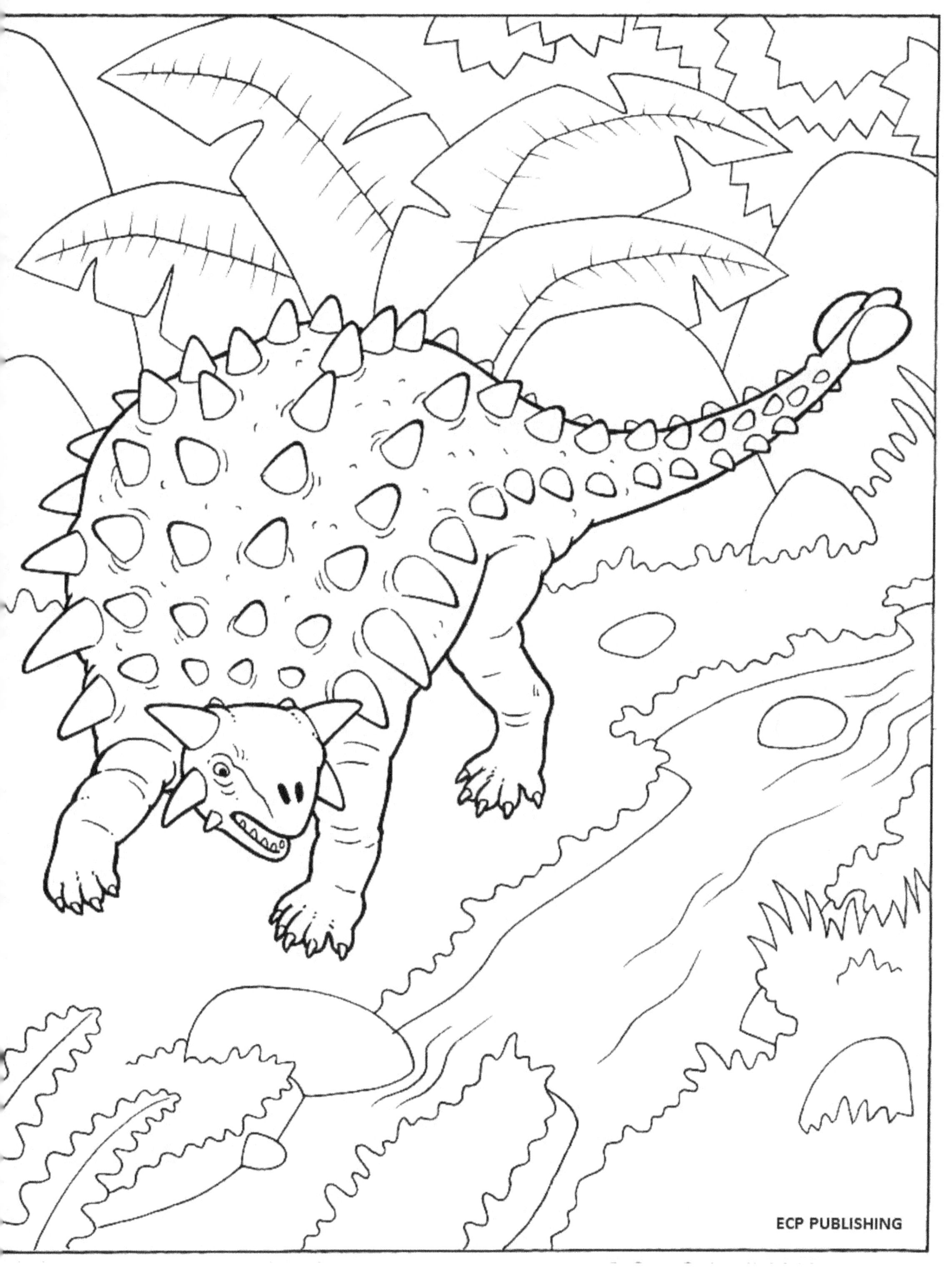
ECP PUBLISHING

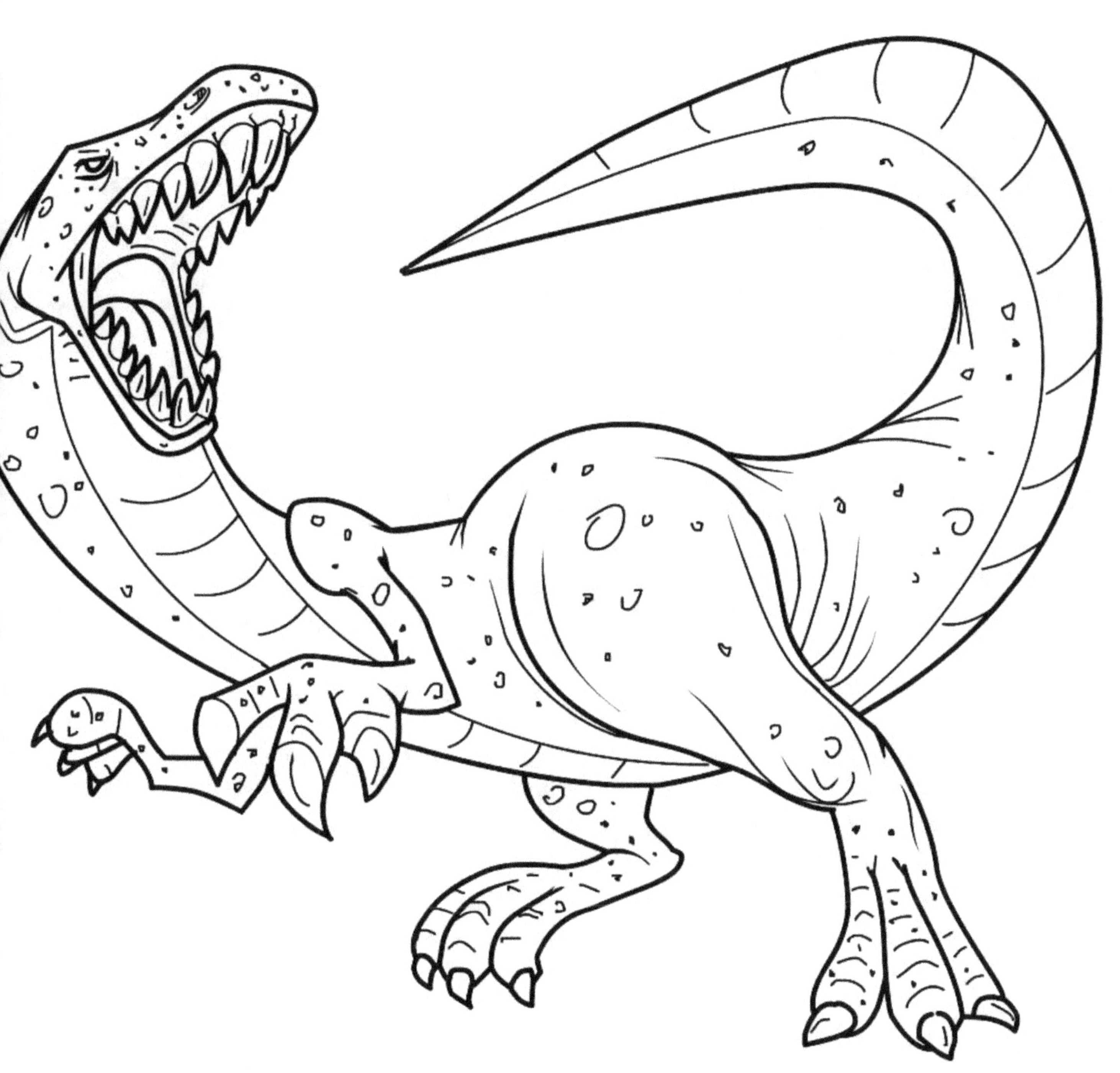

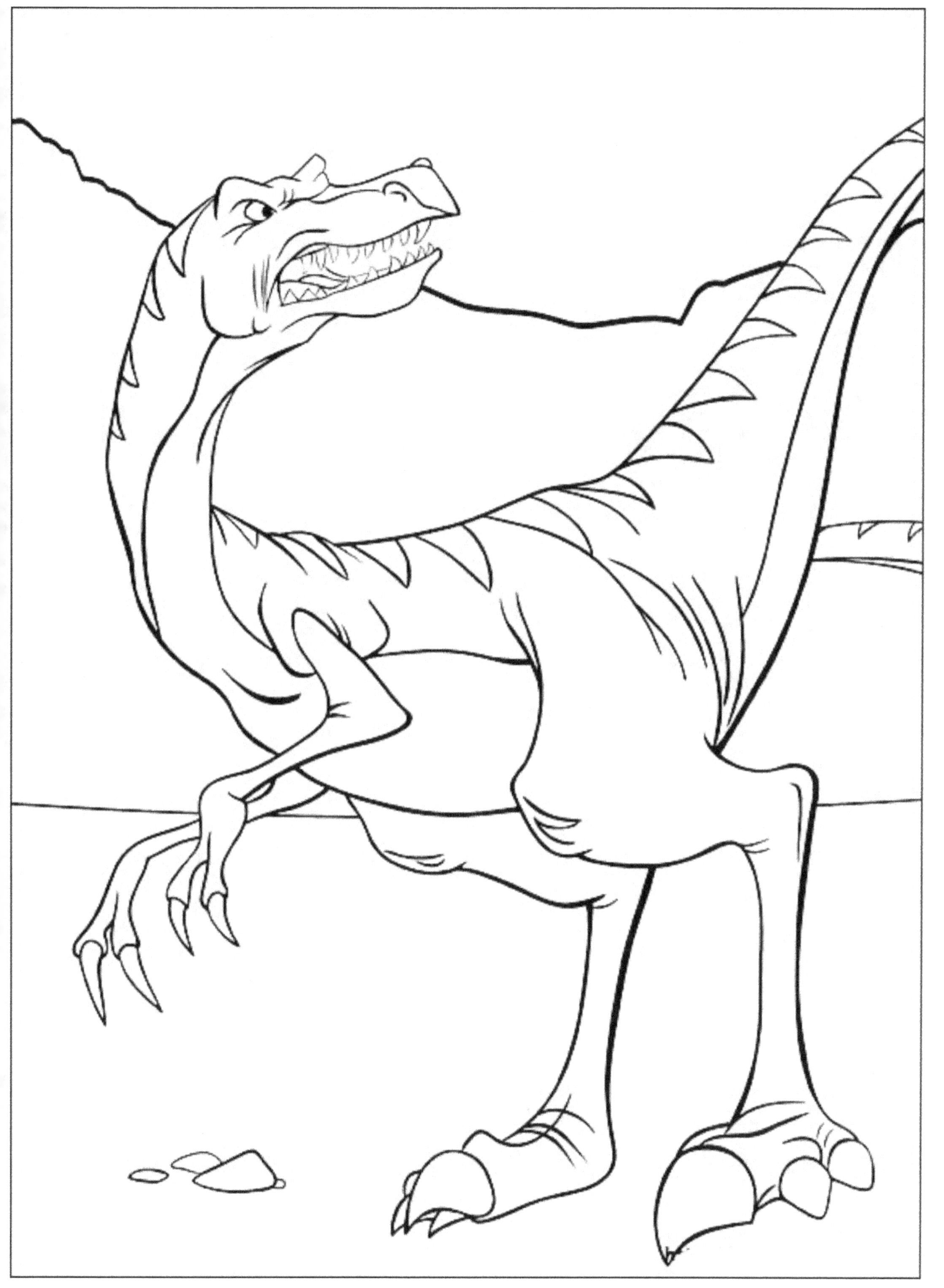

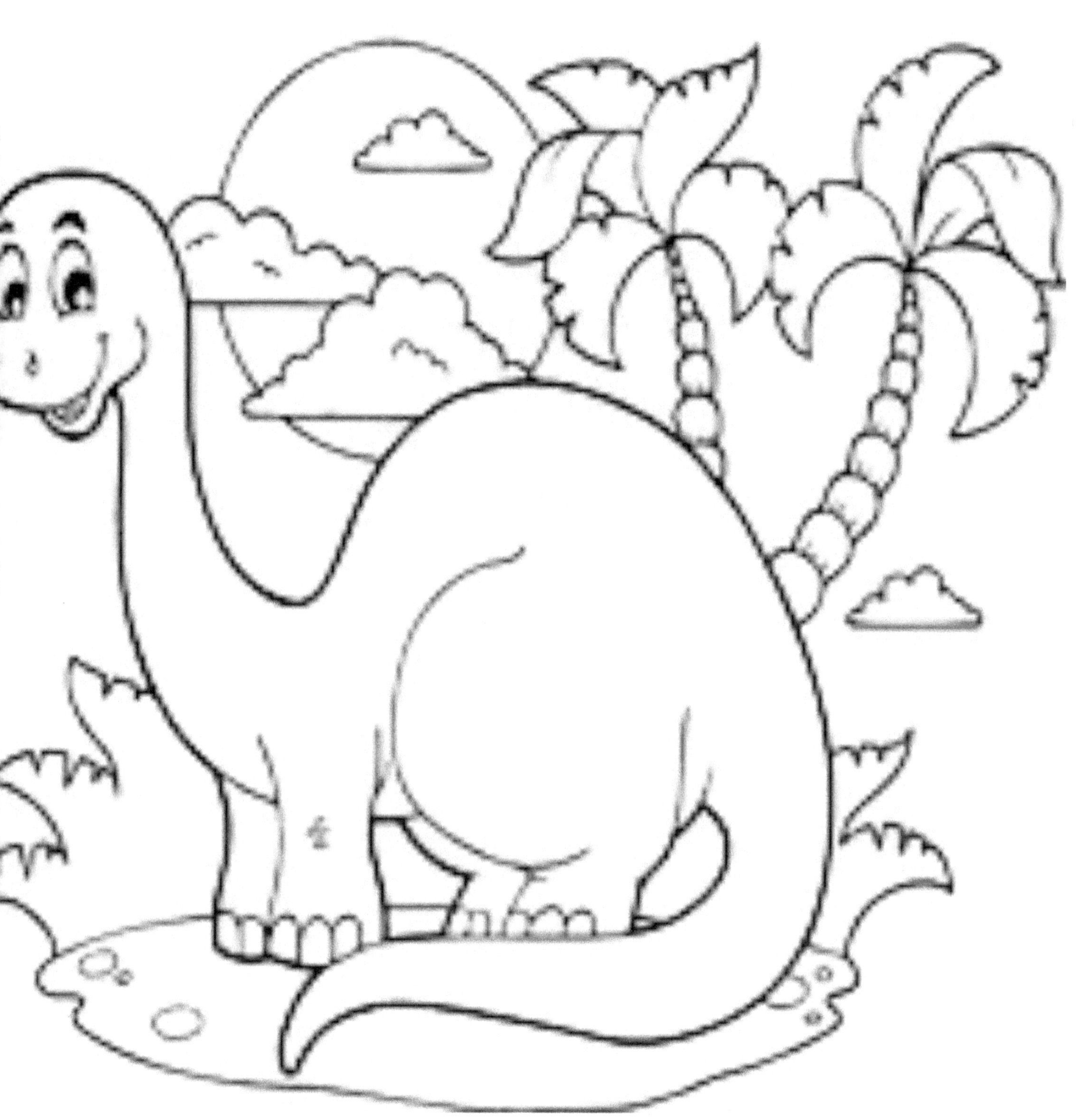

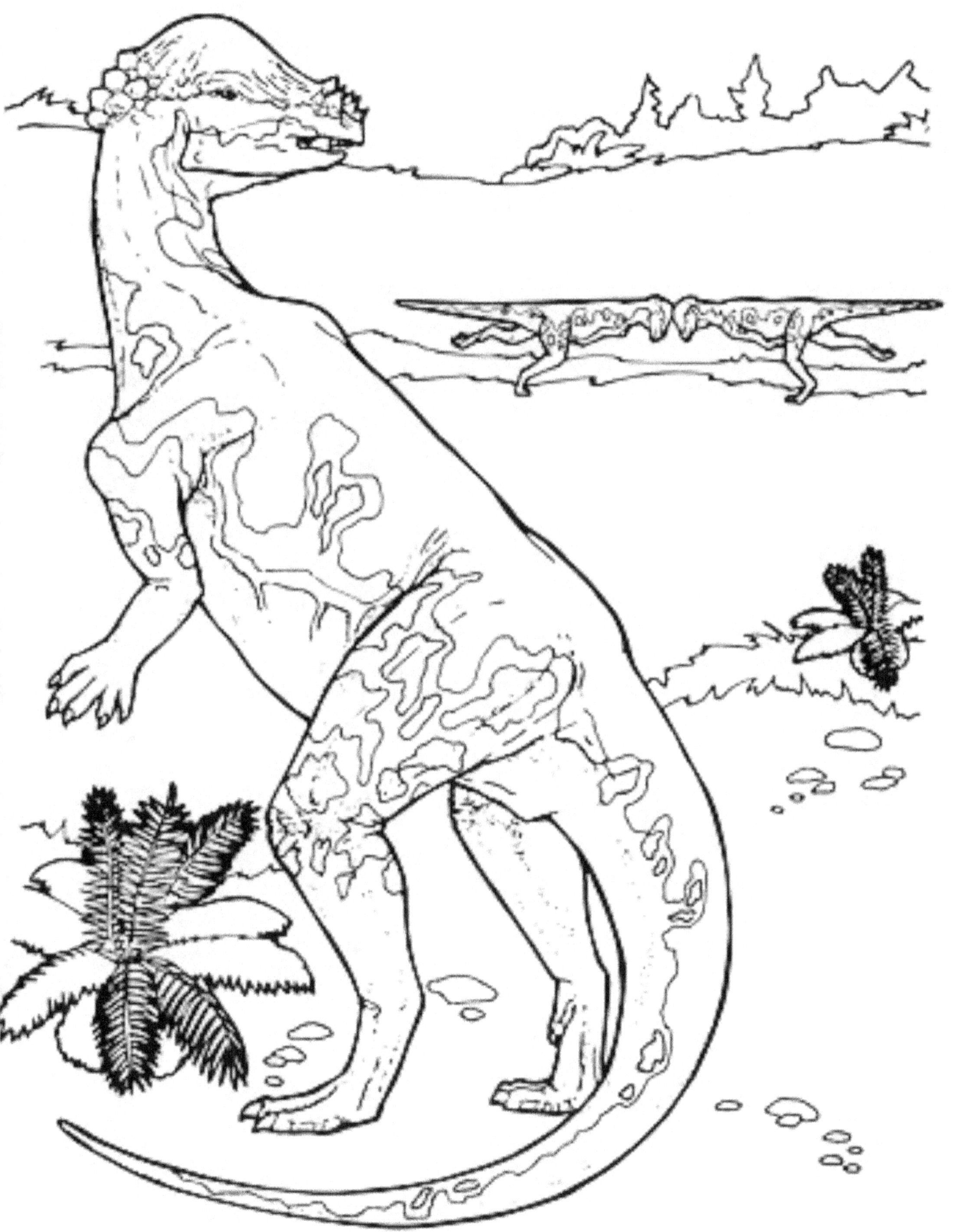

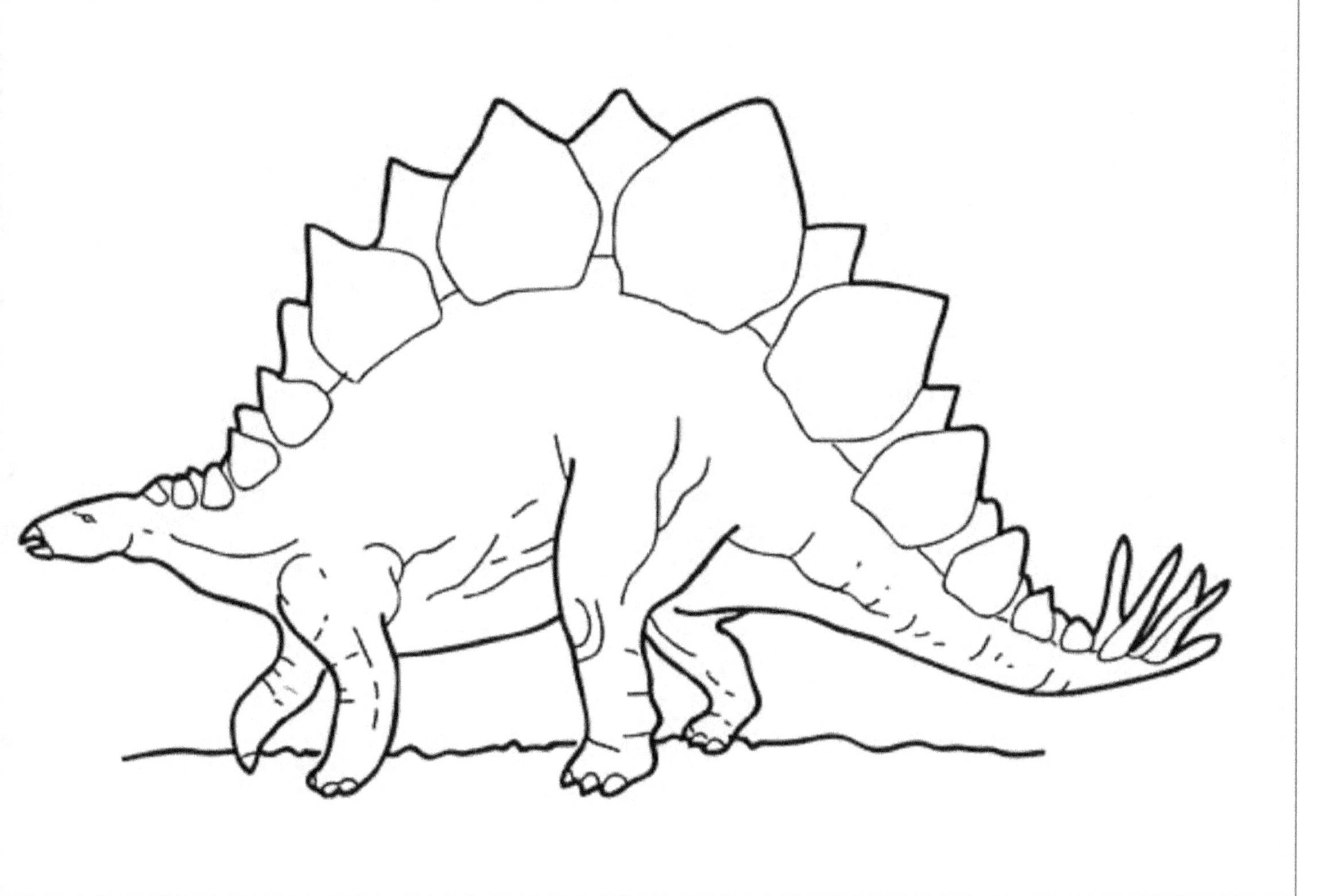

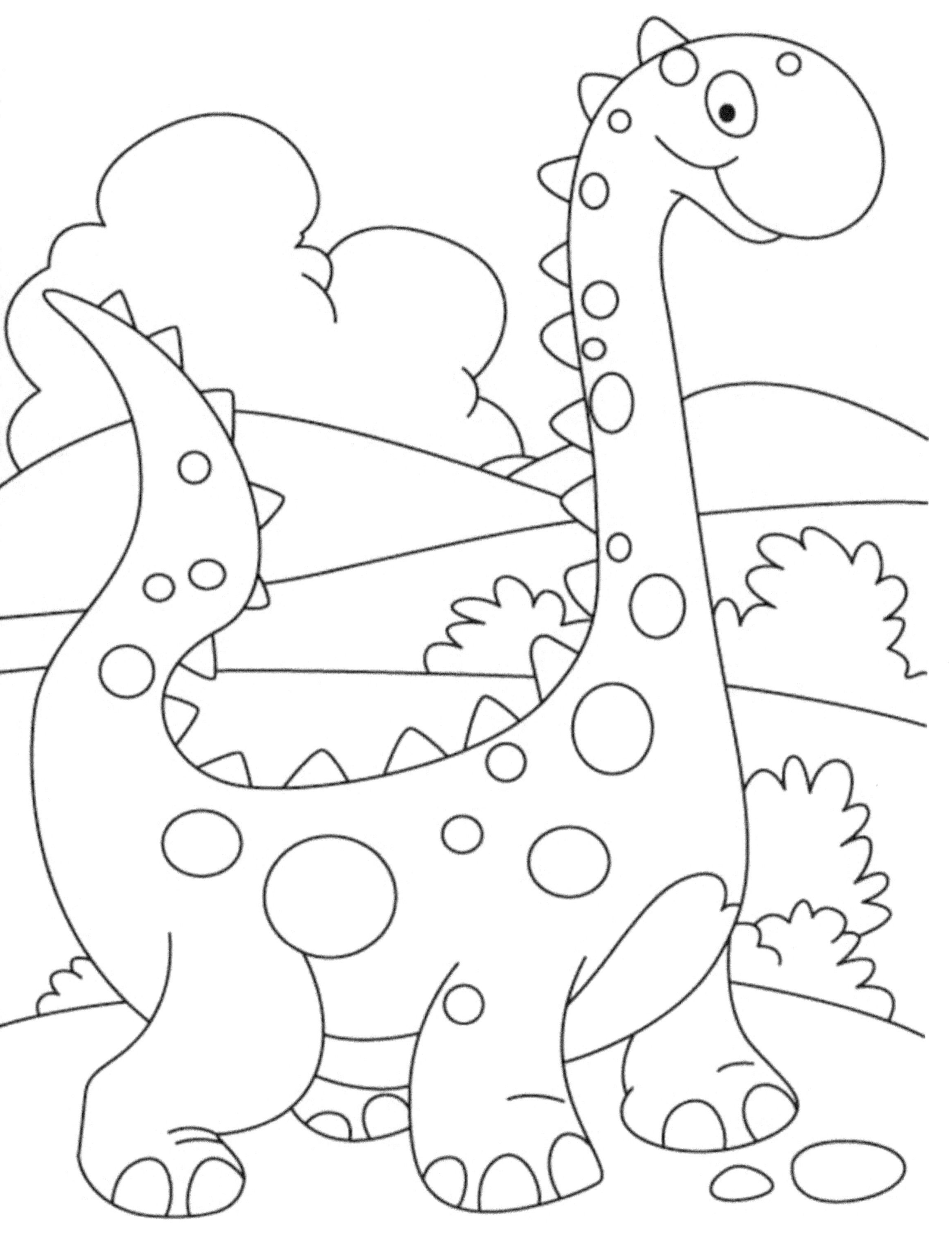

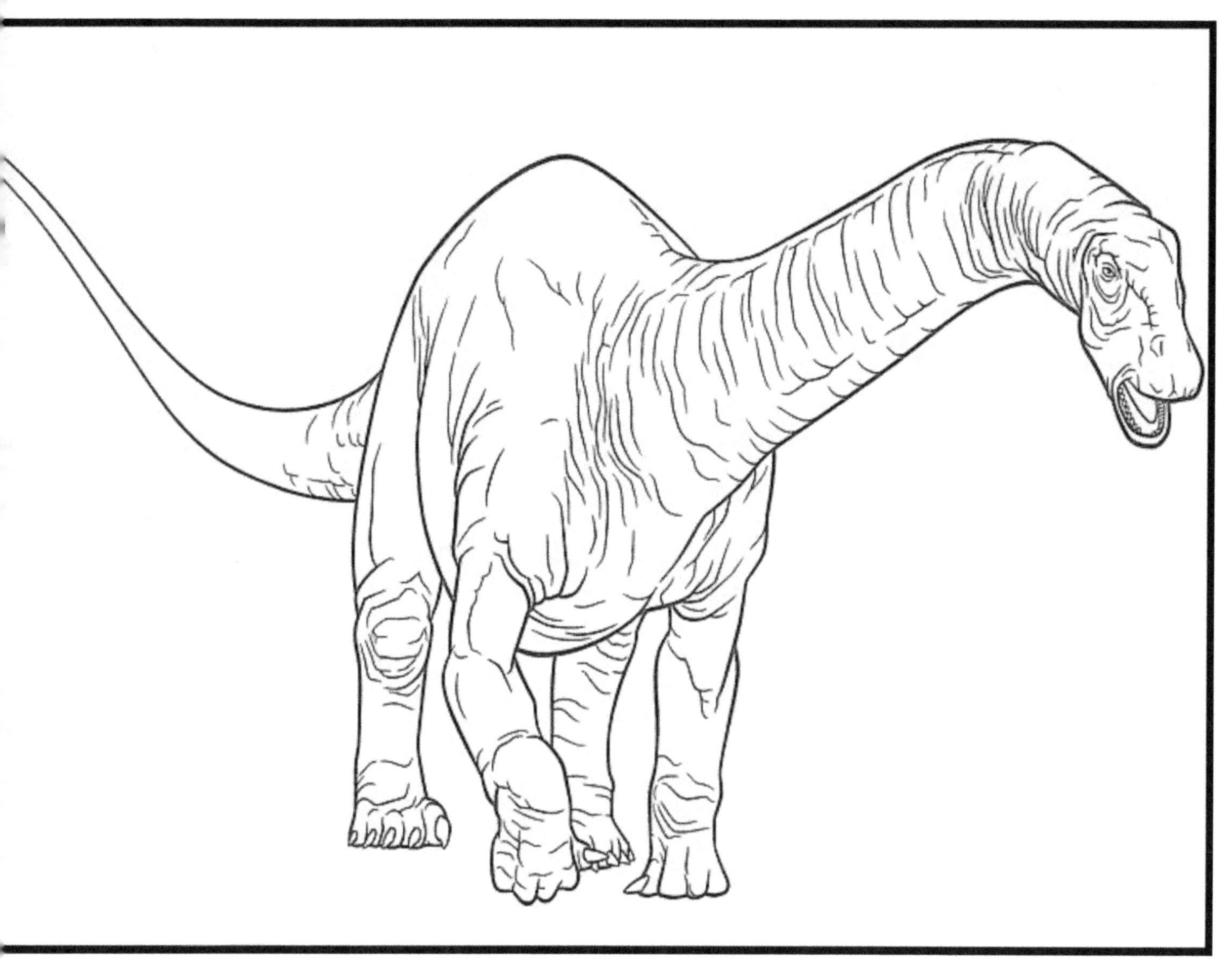

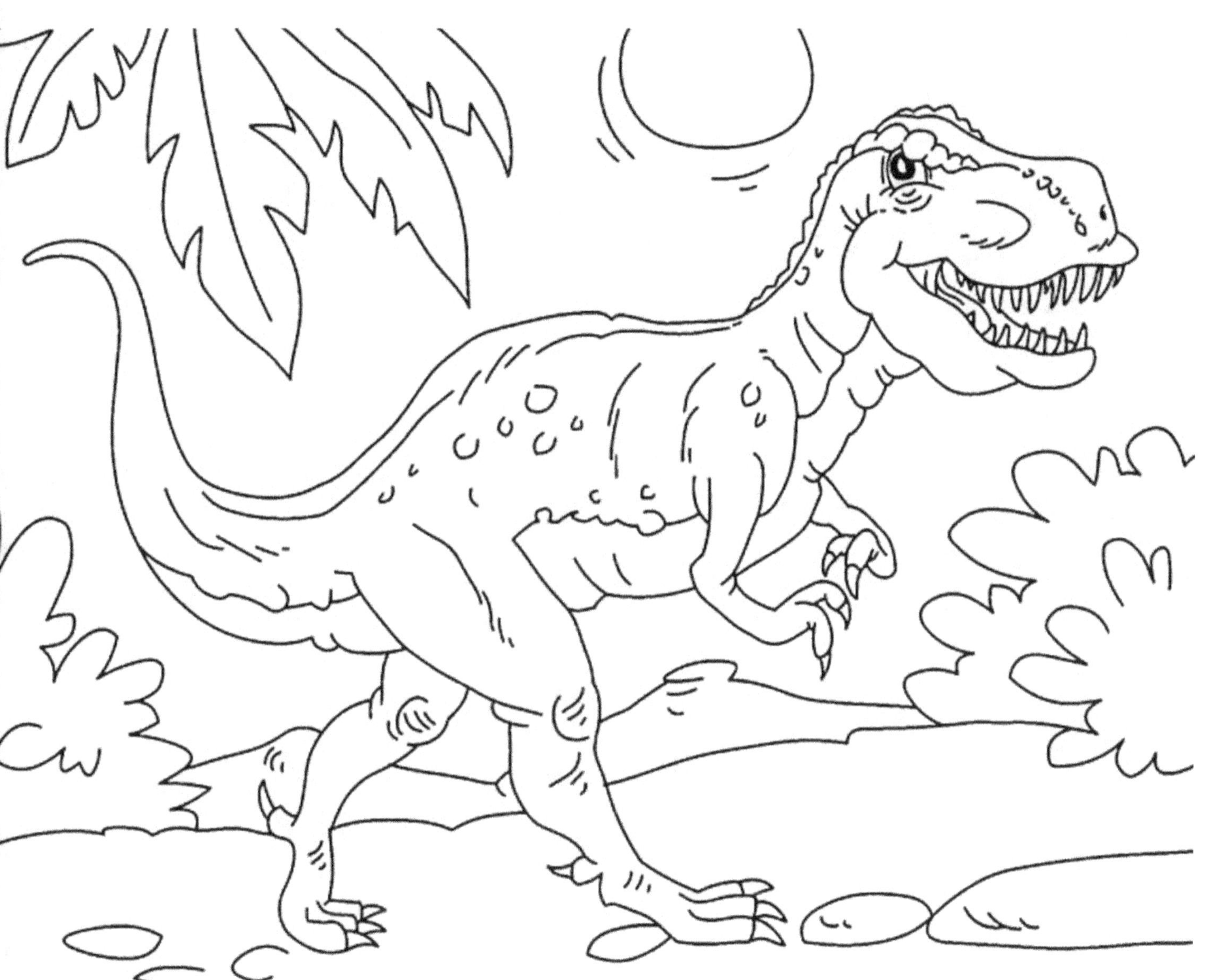

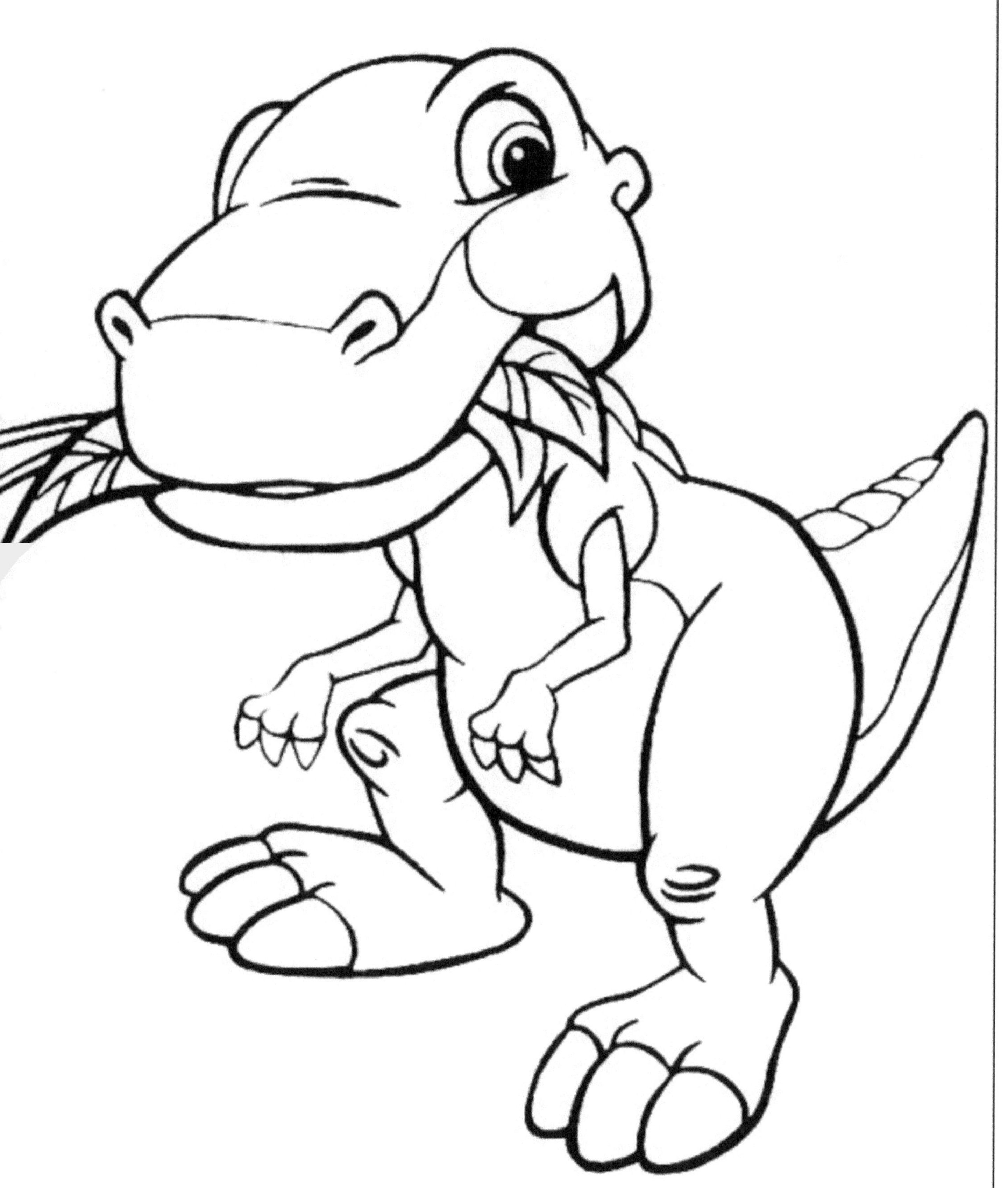

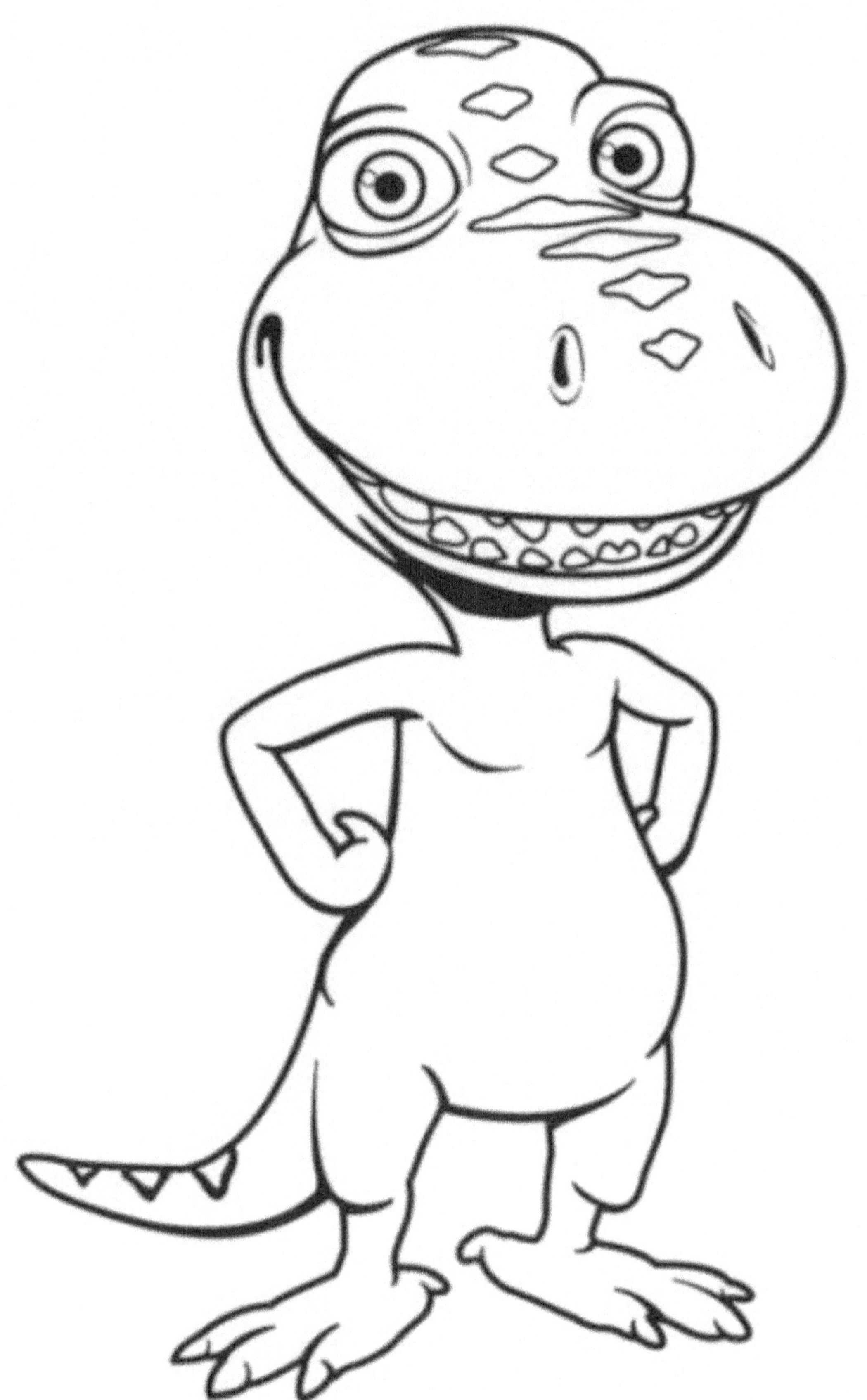

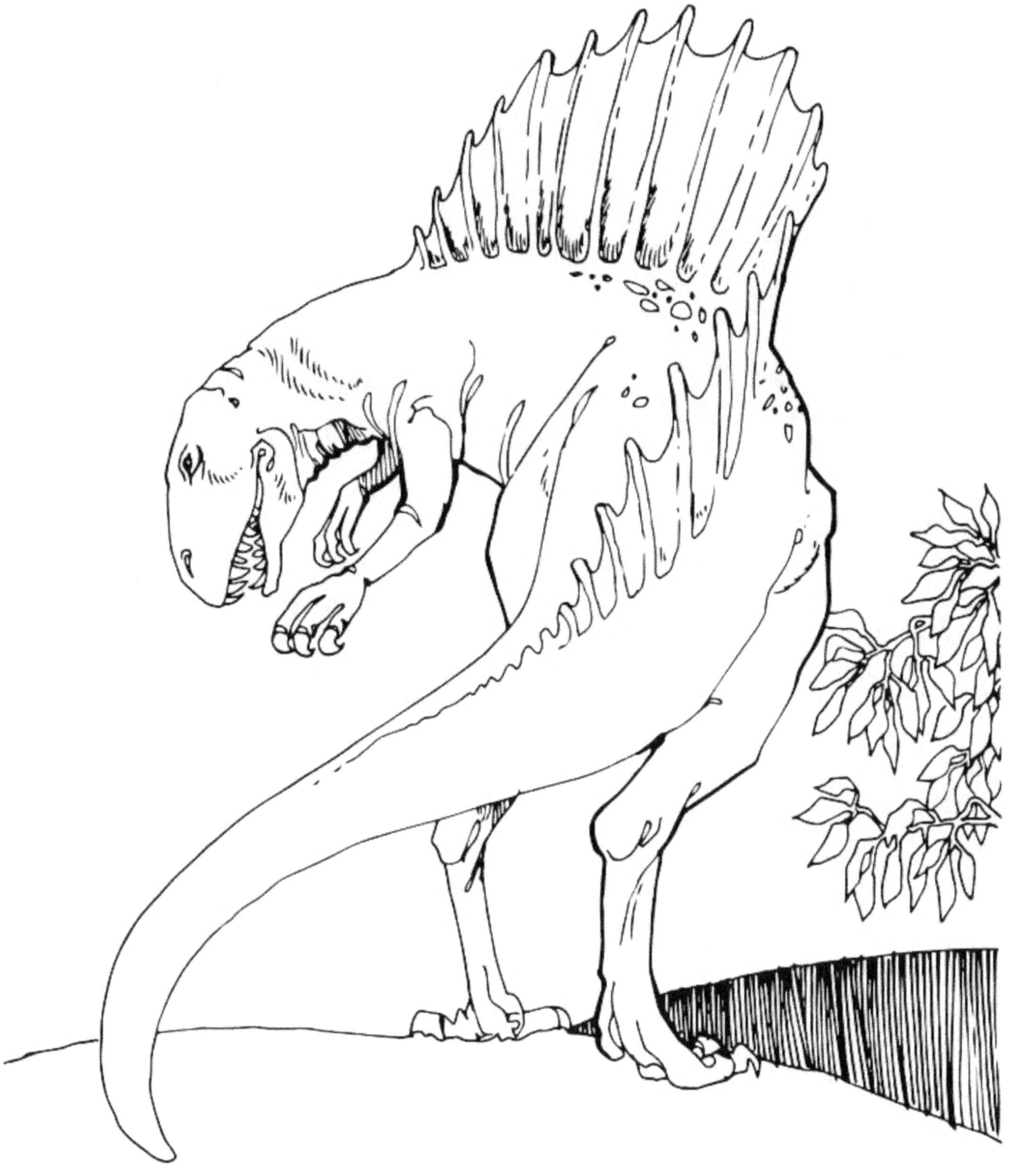

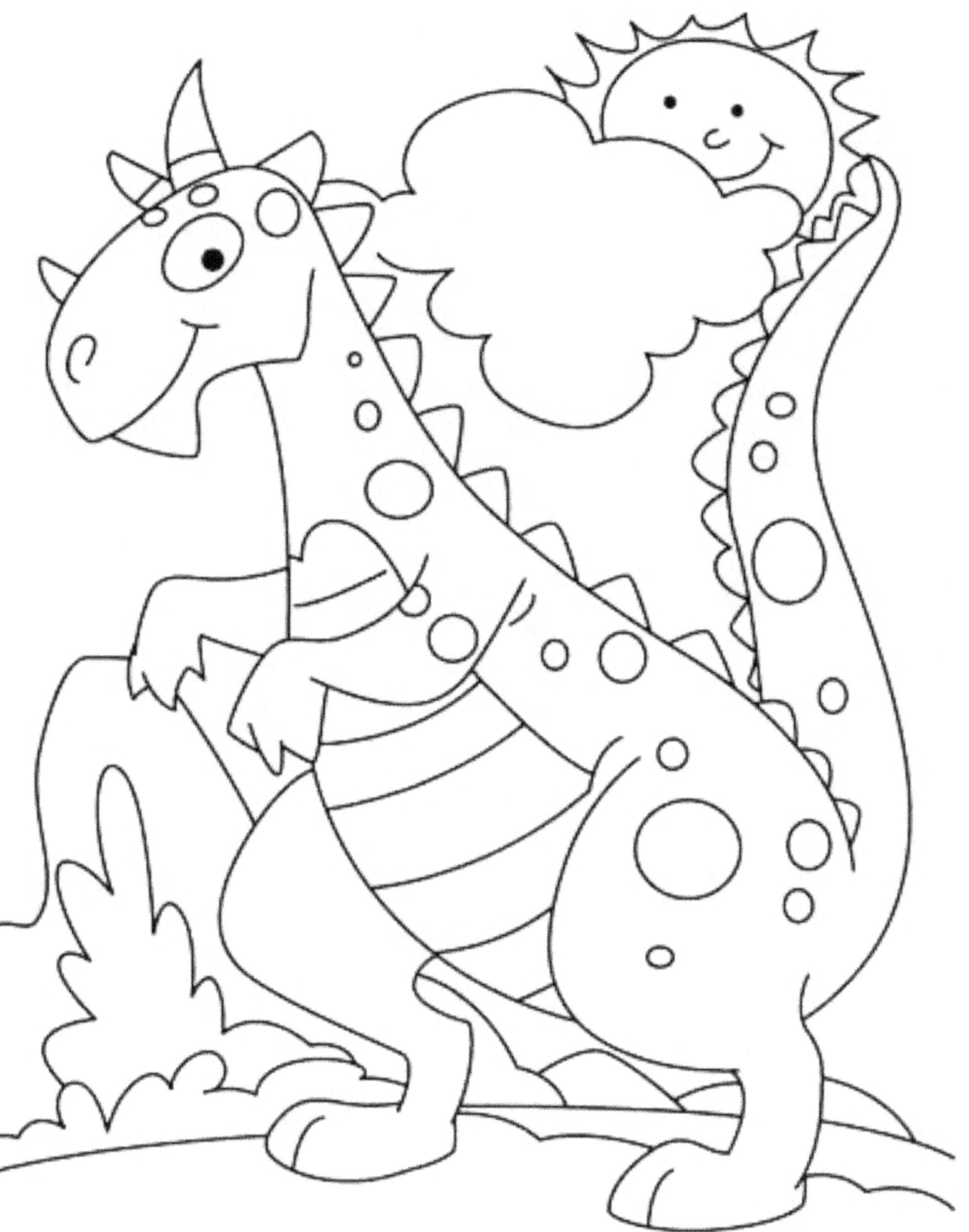

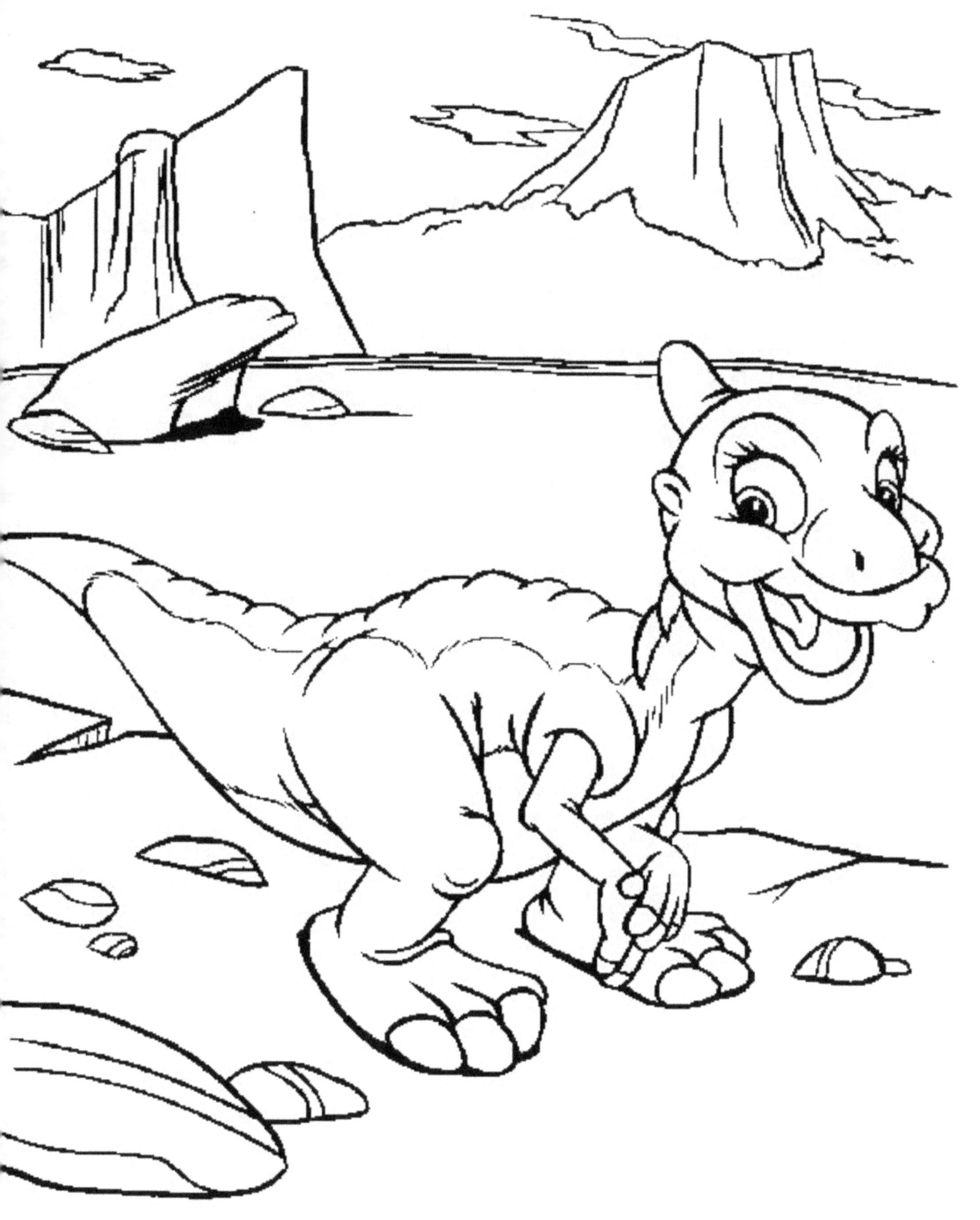

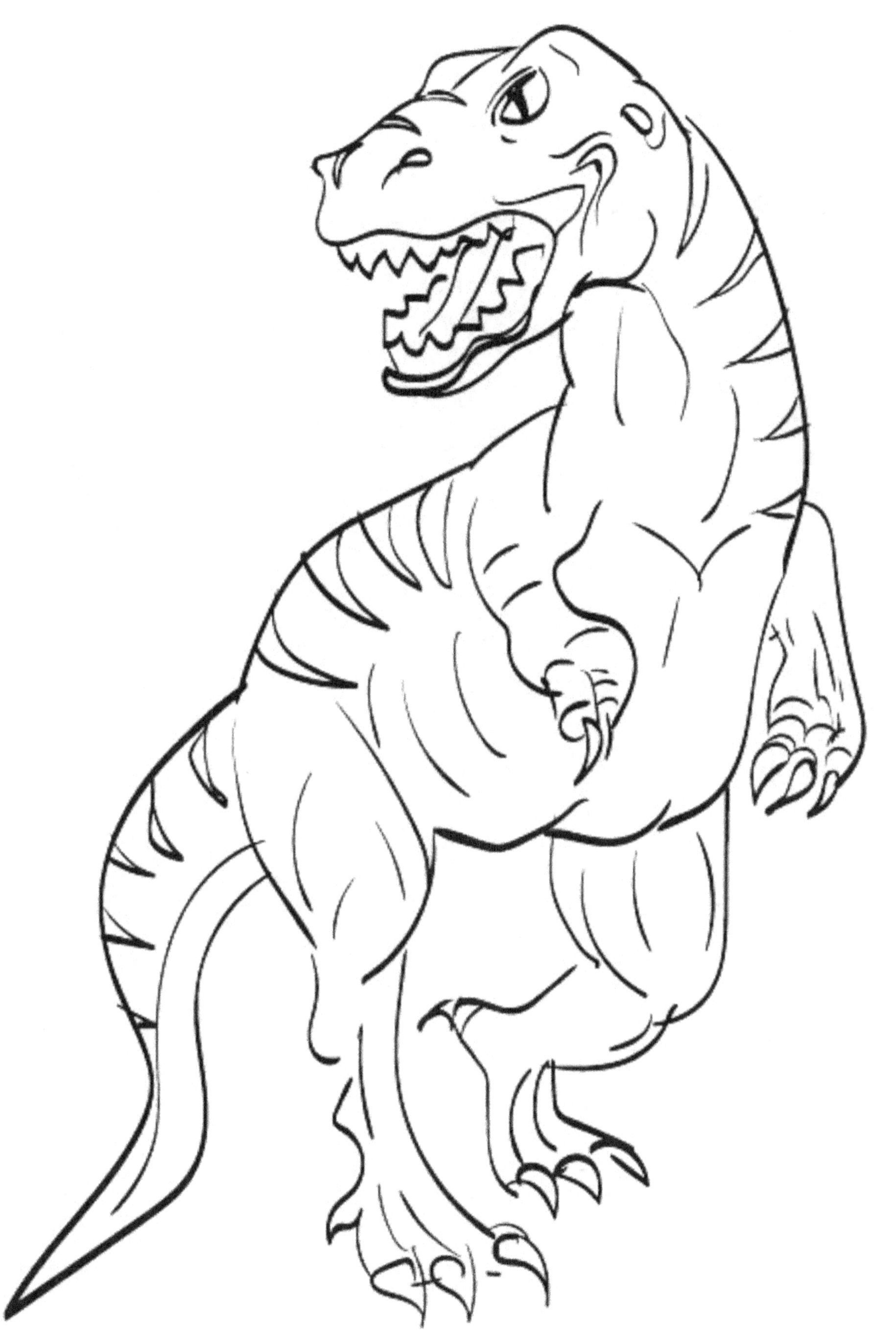

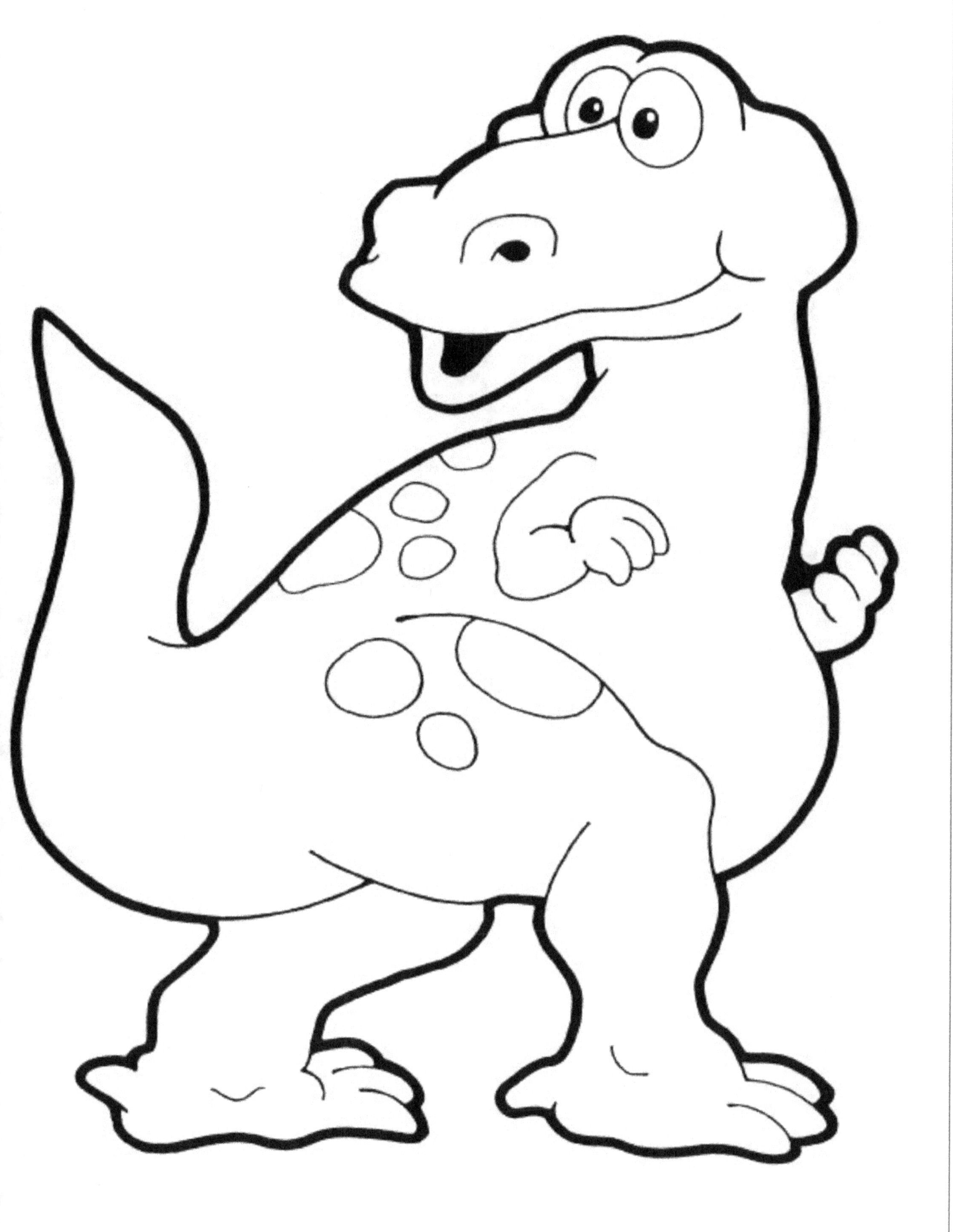

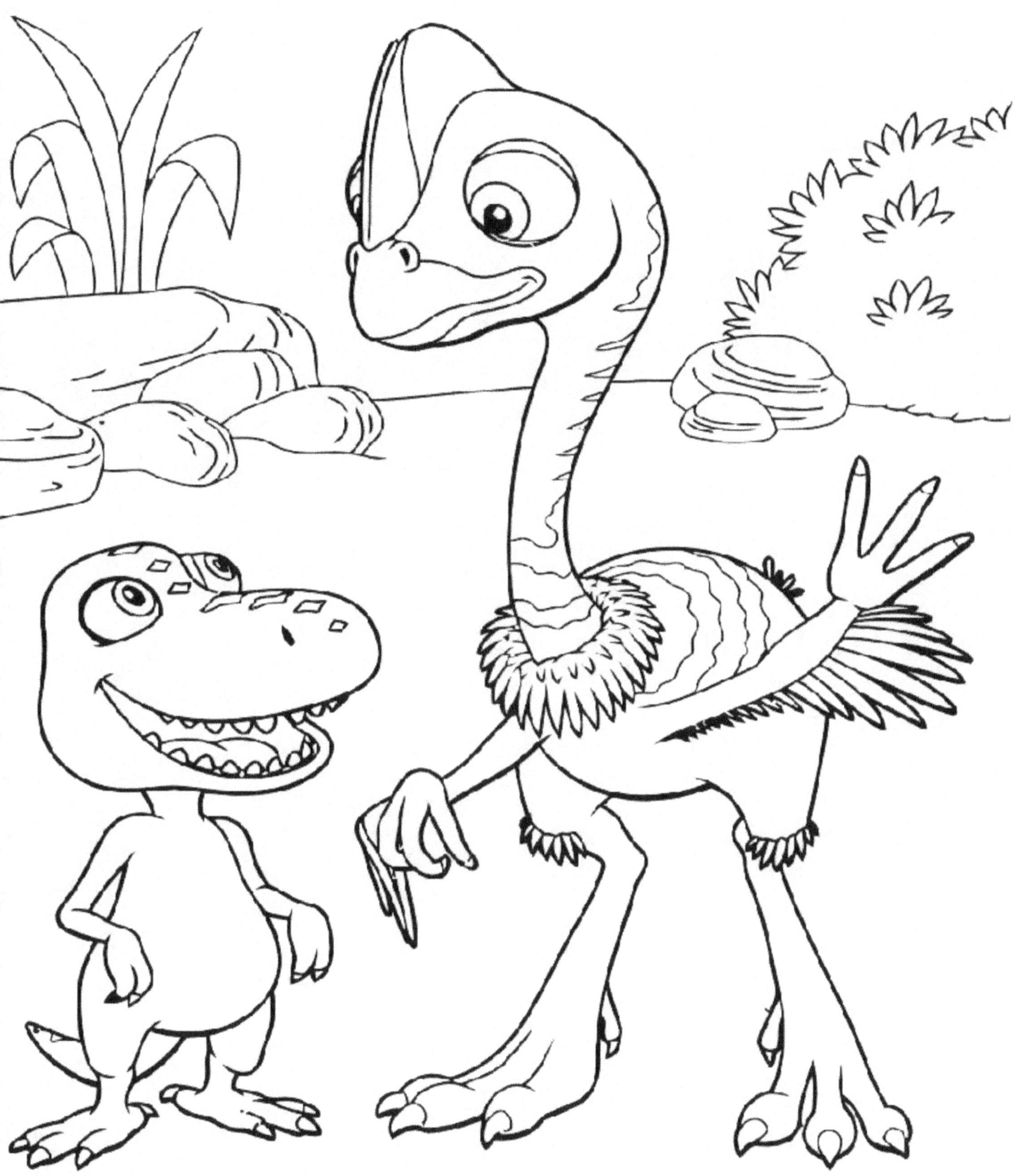

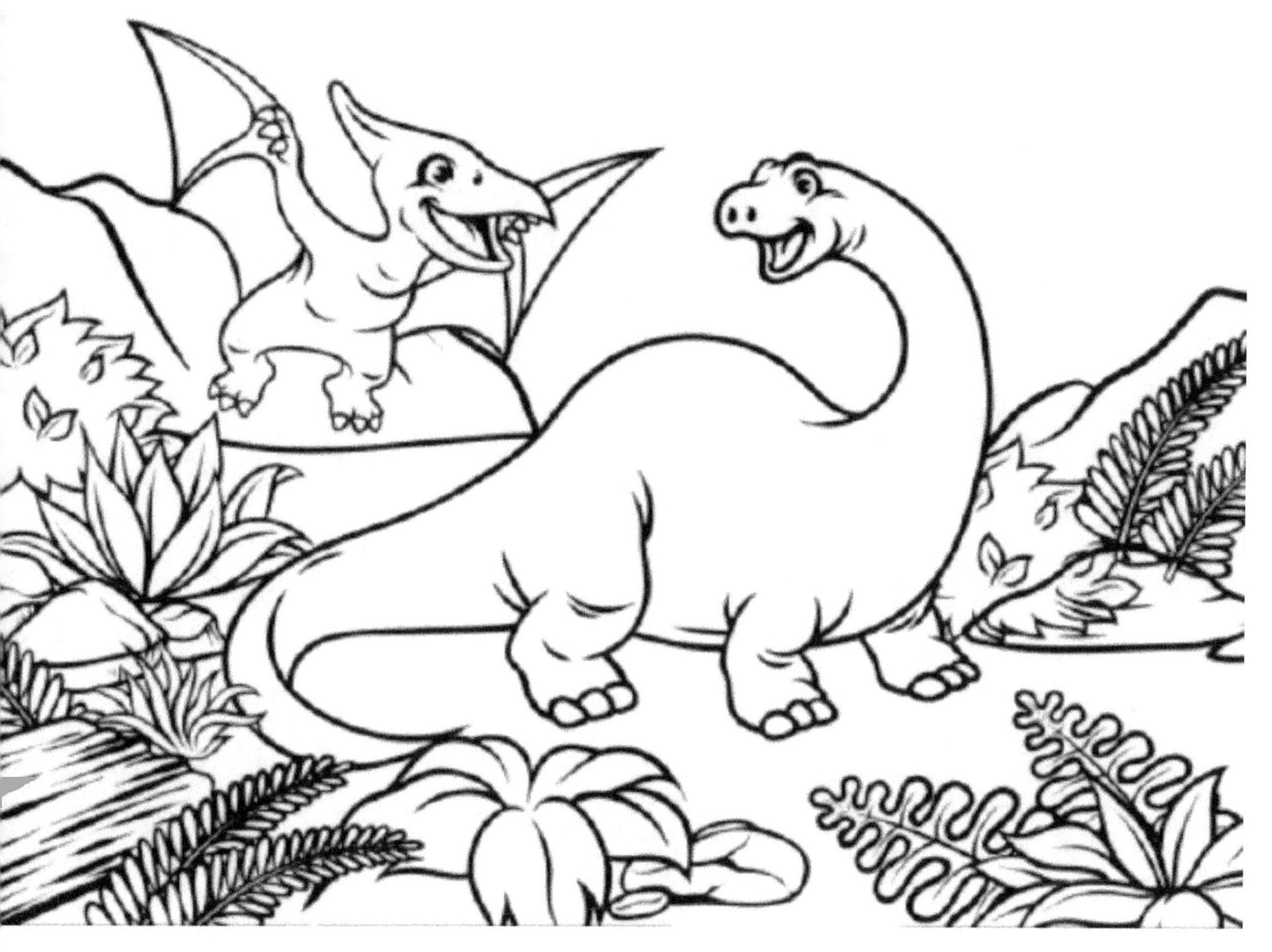

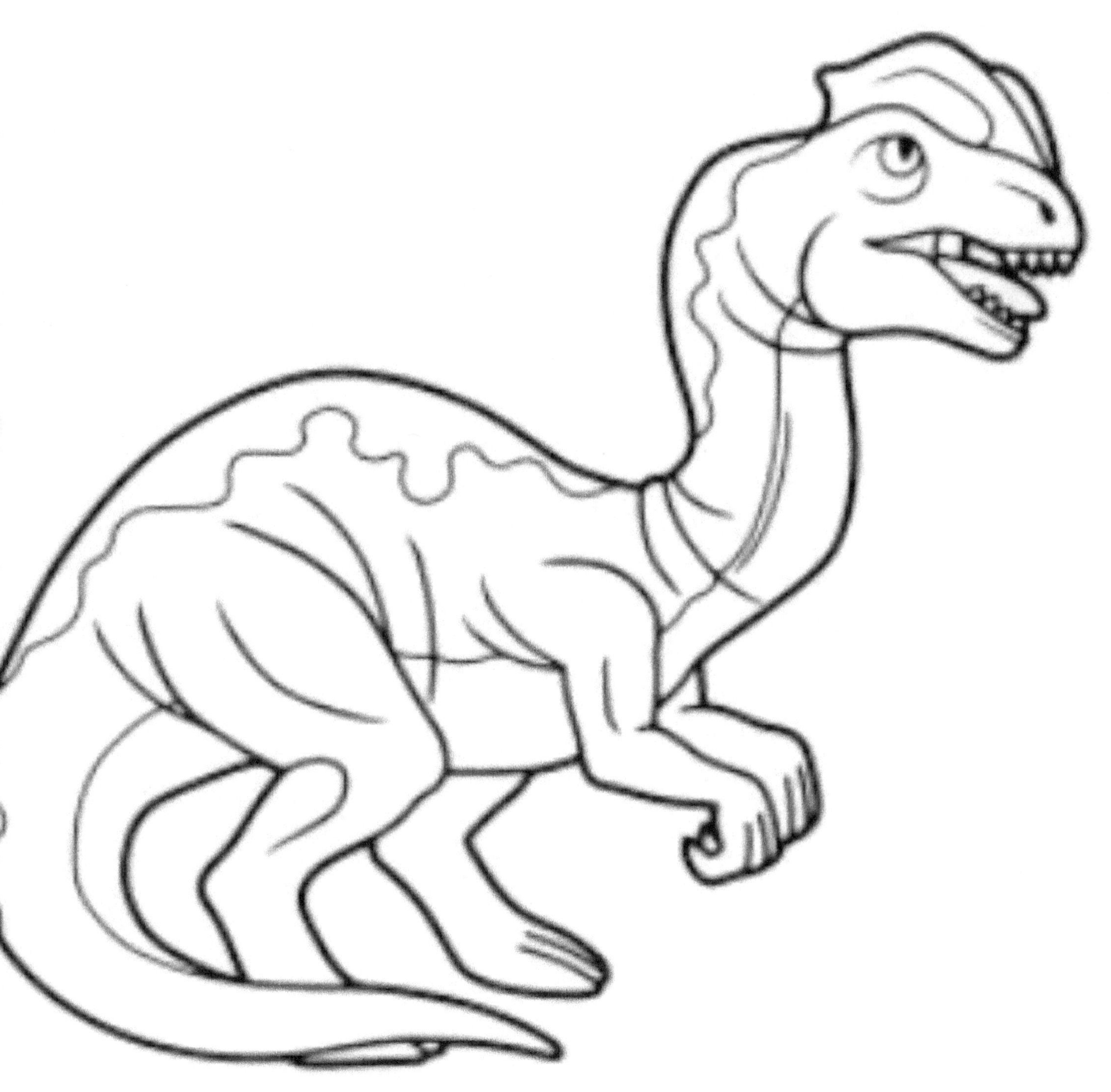

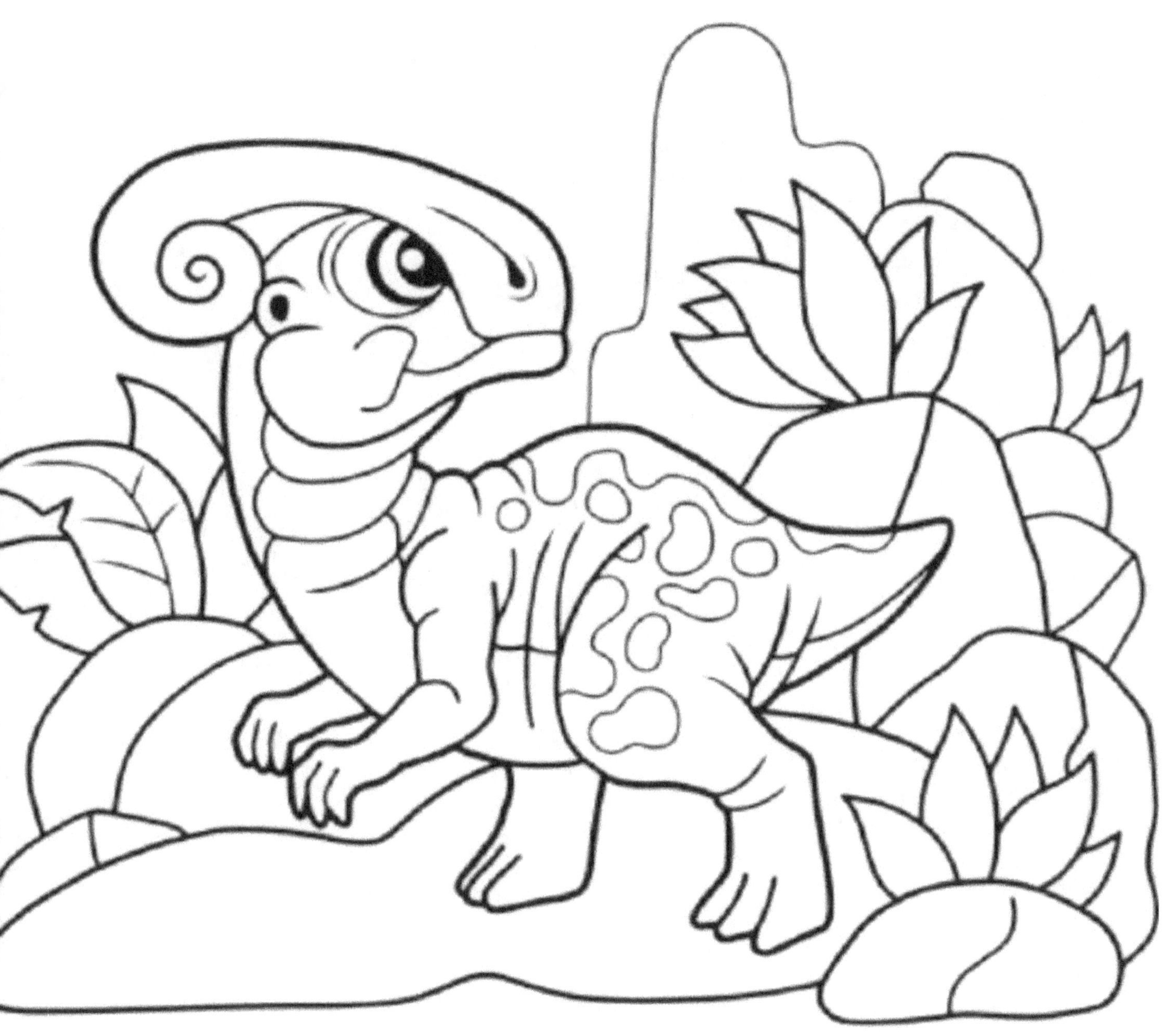

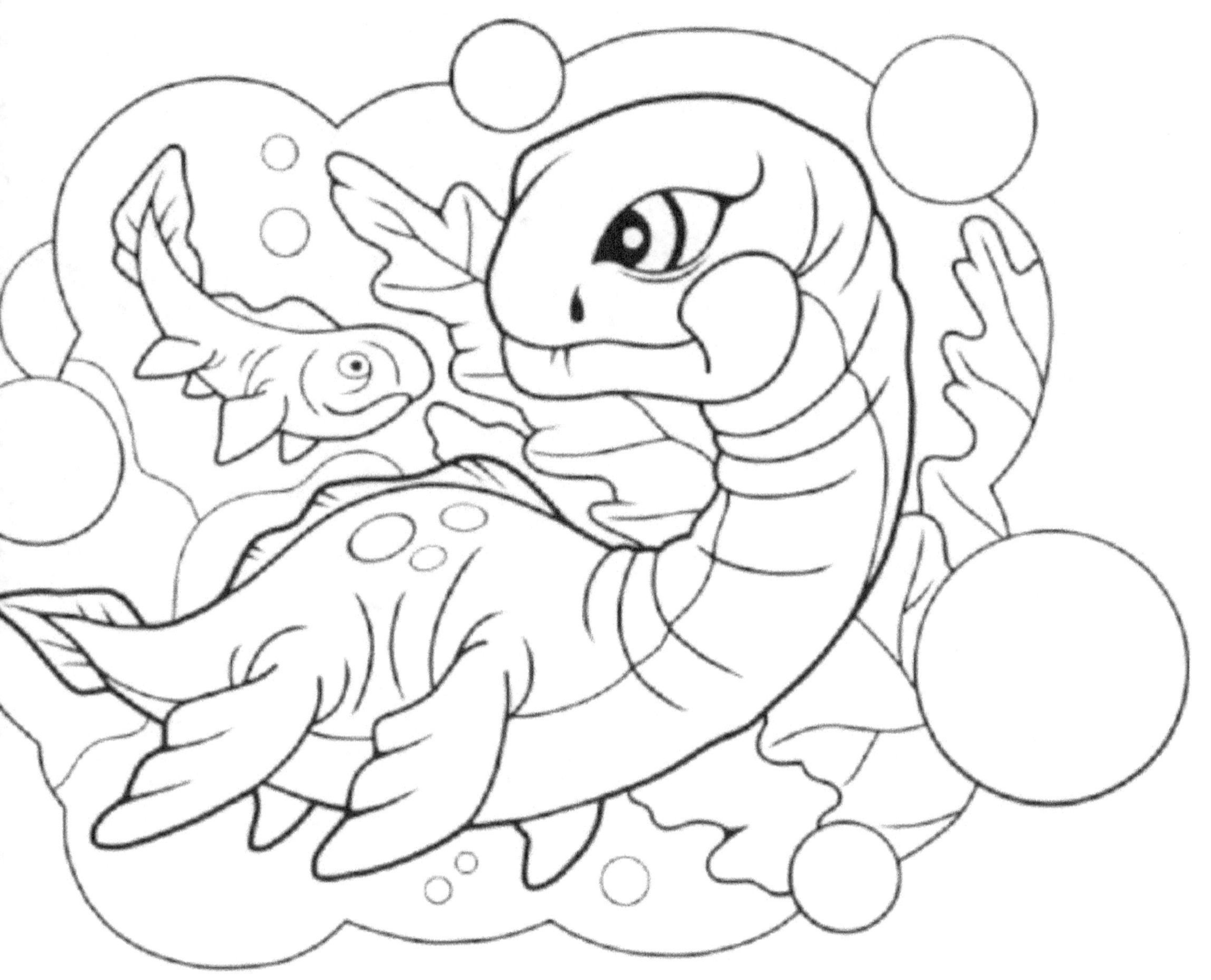

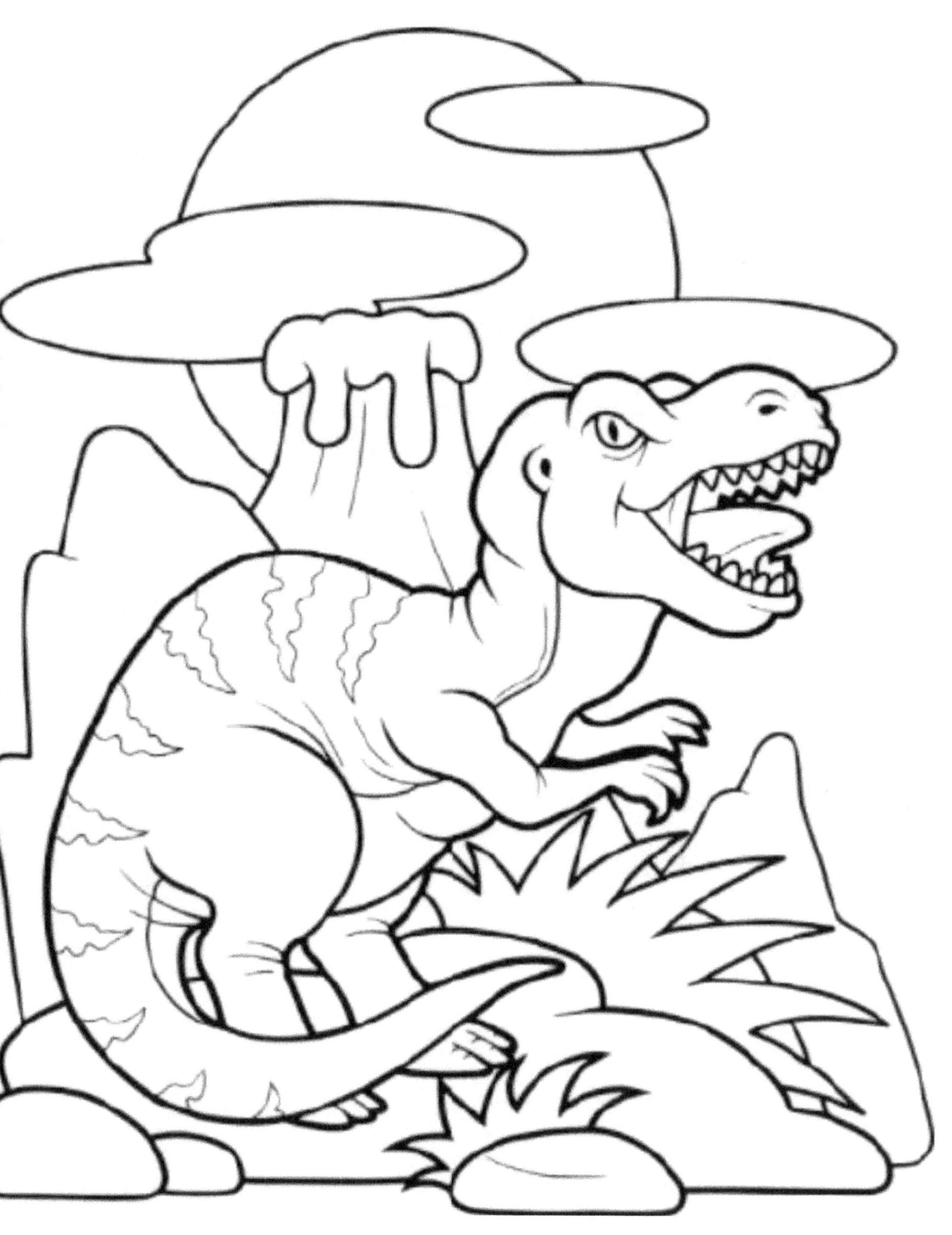

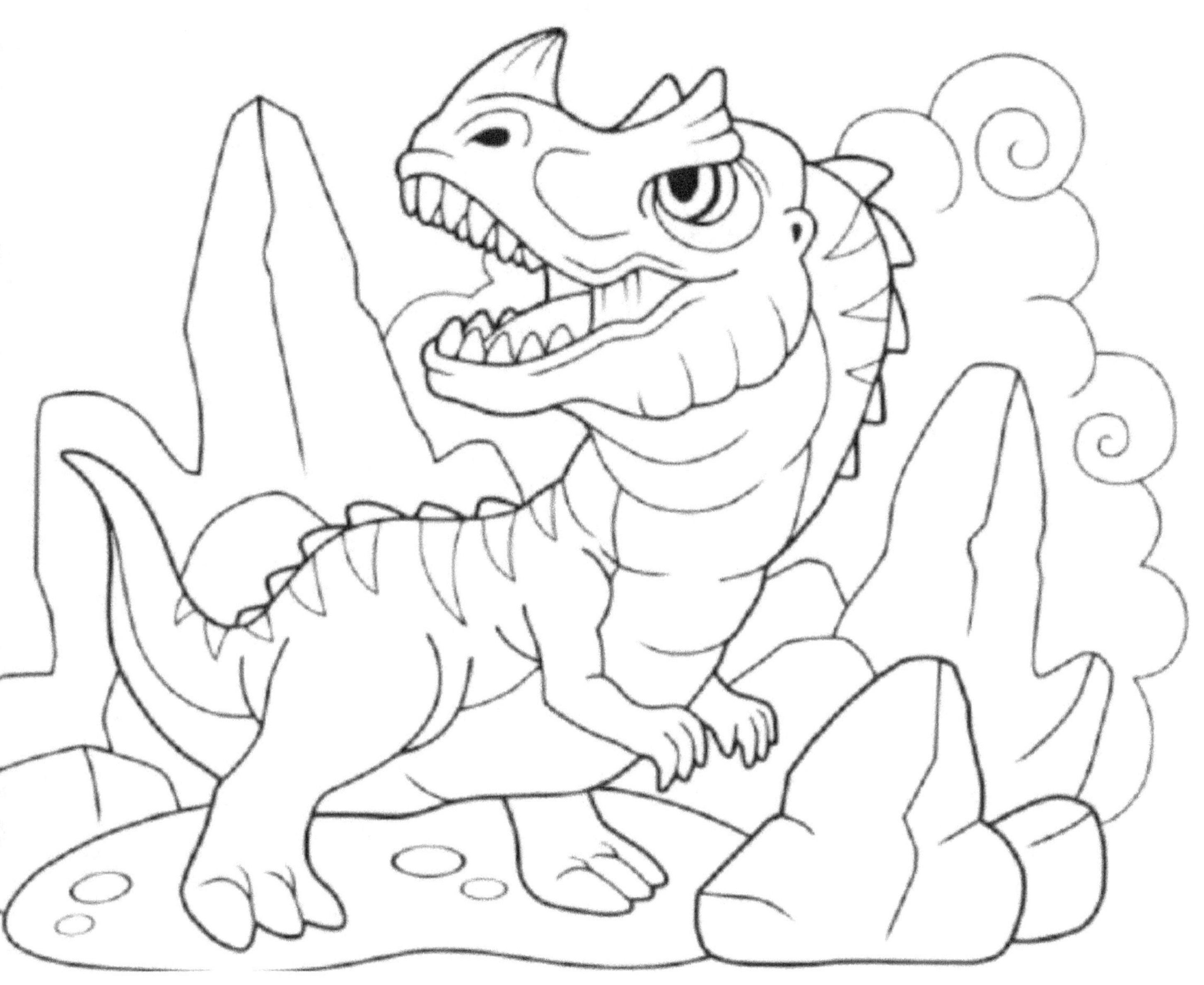

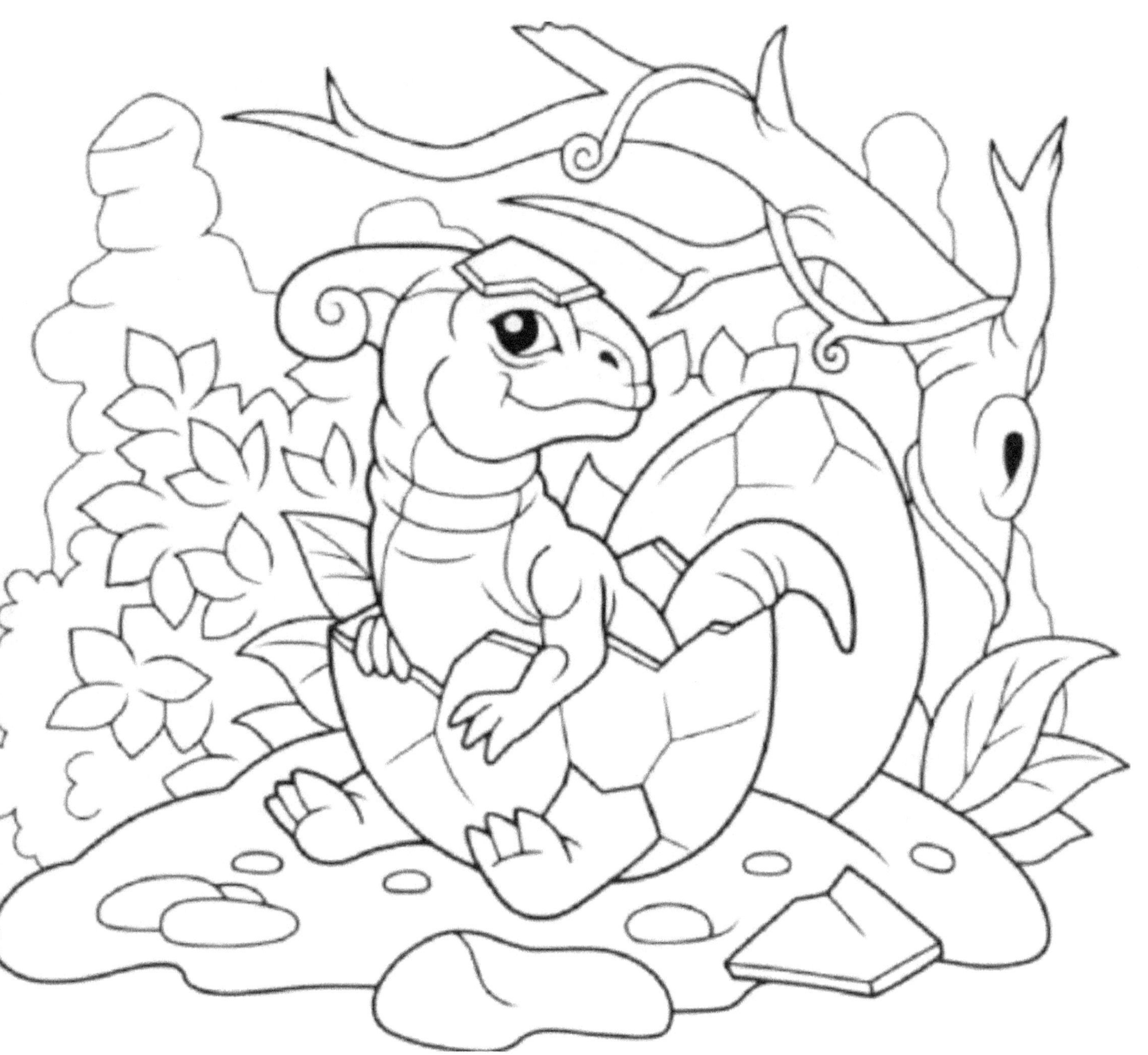

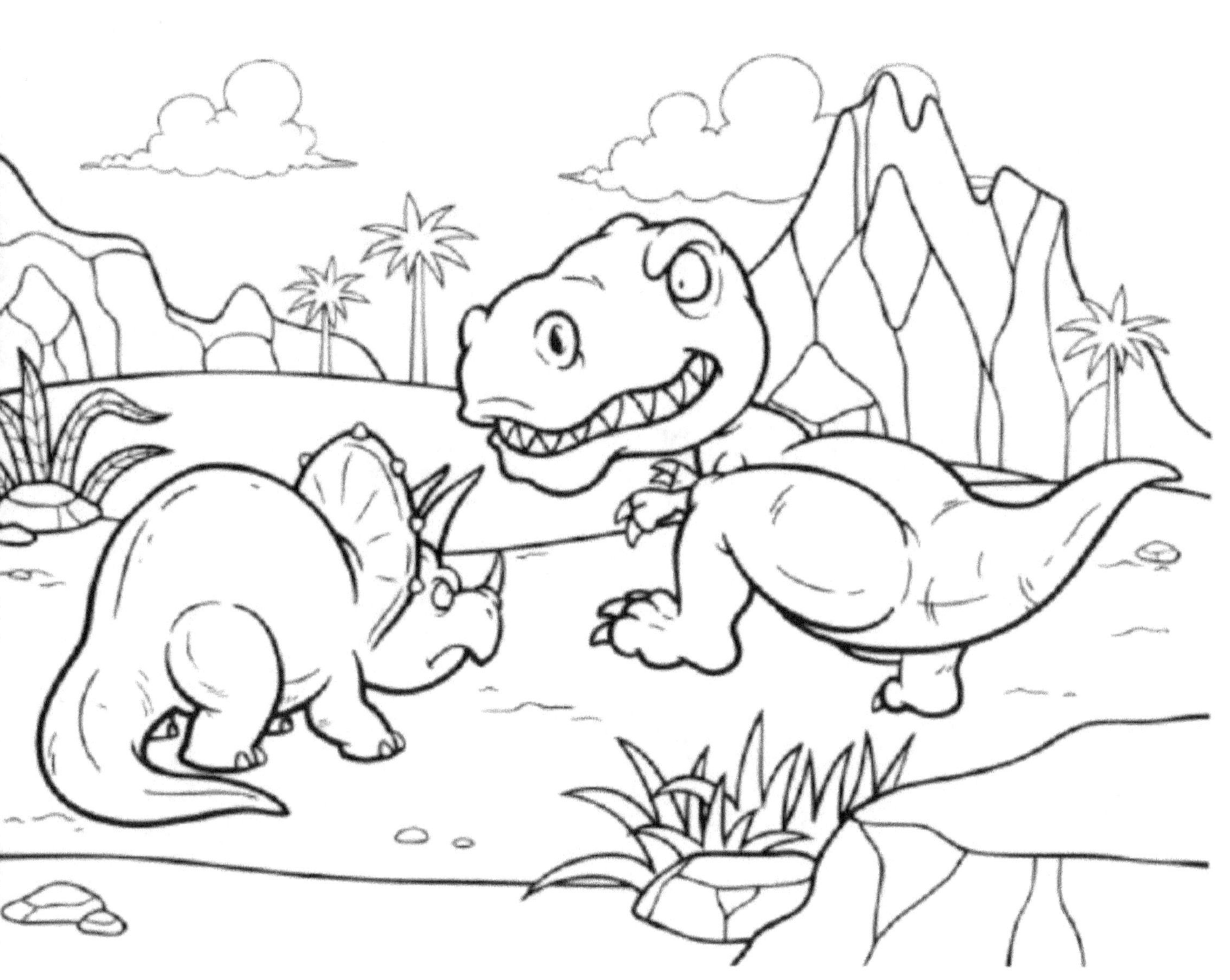

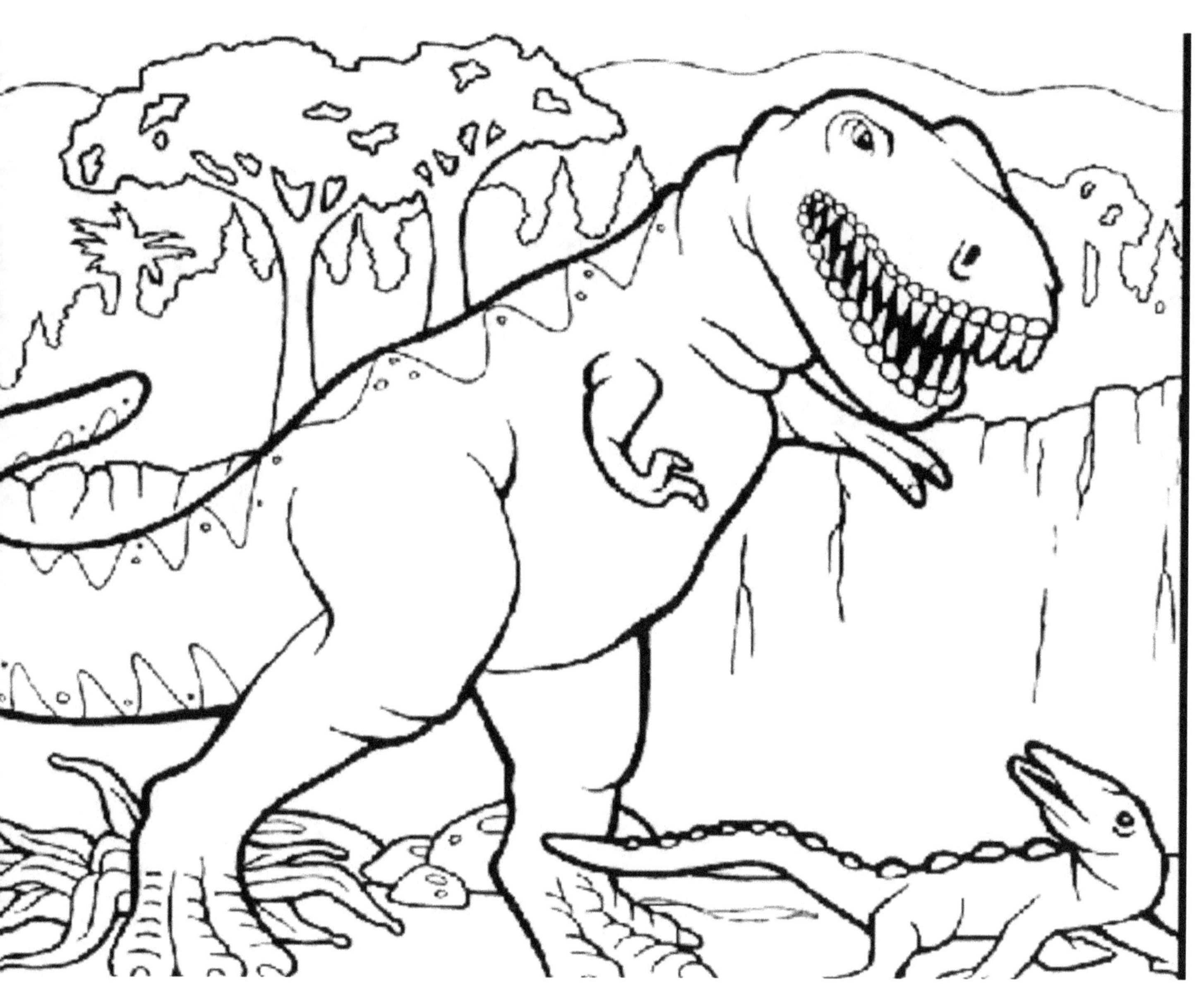

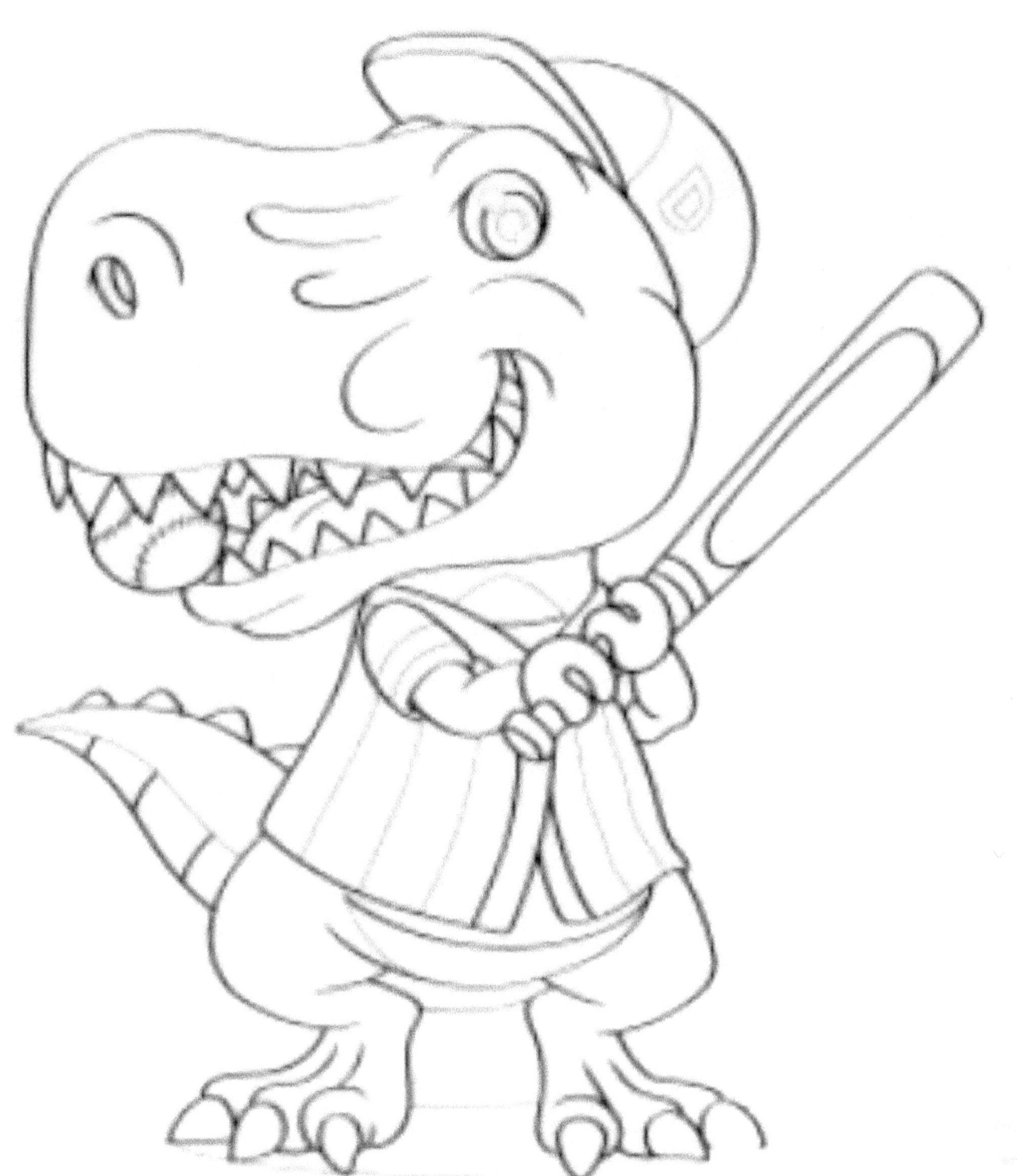

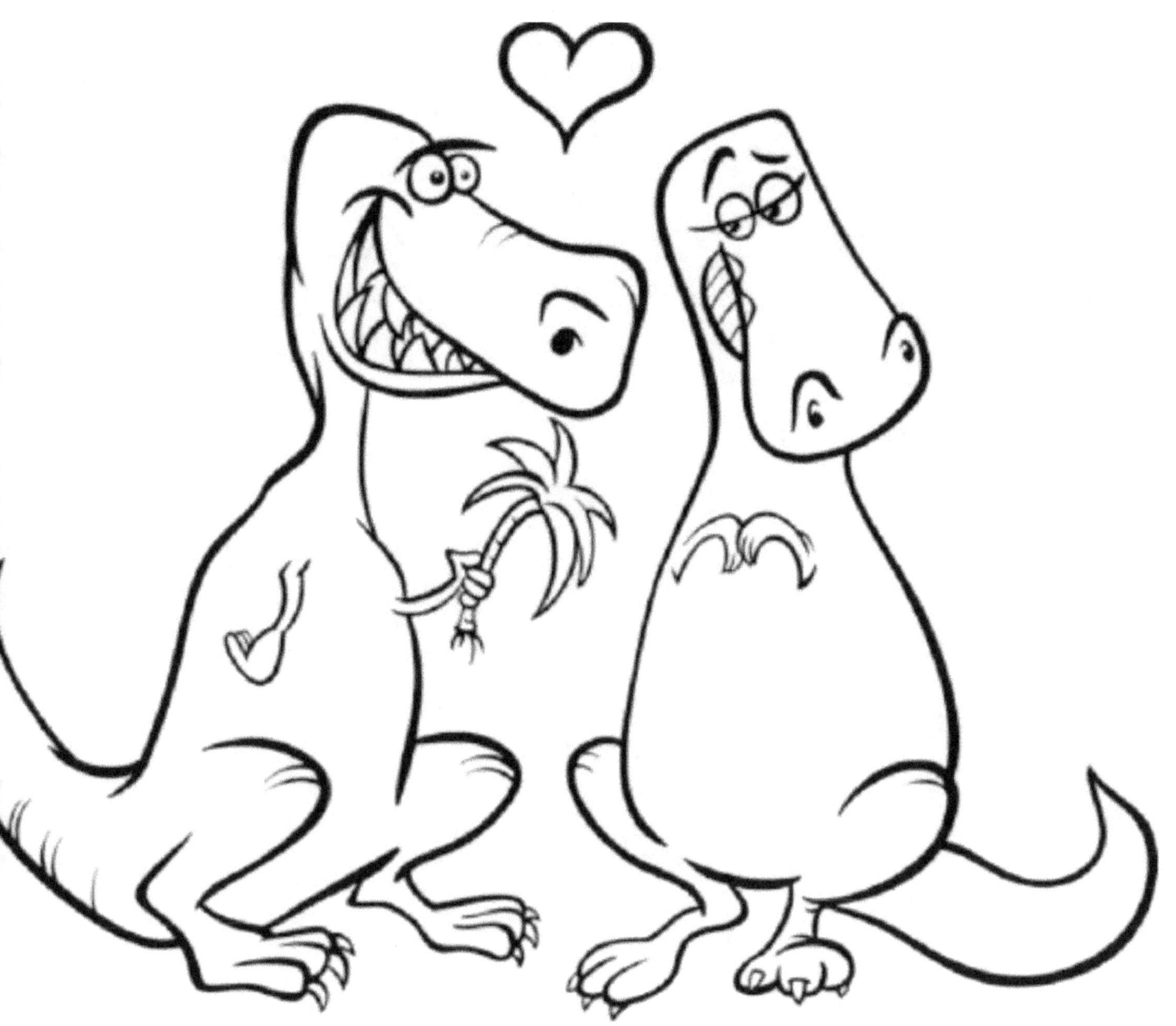

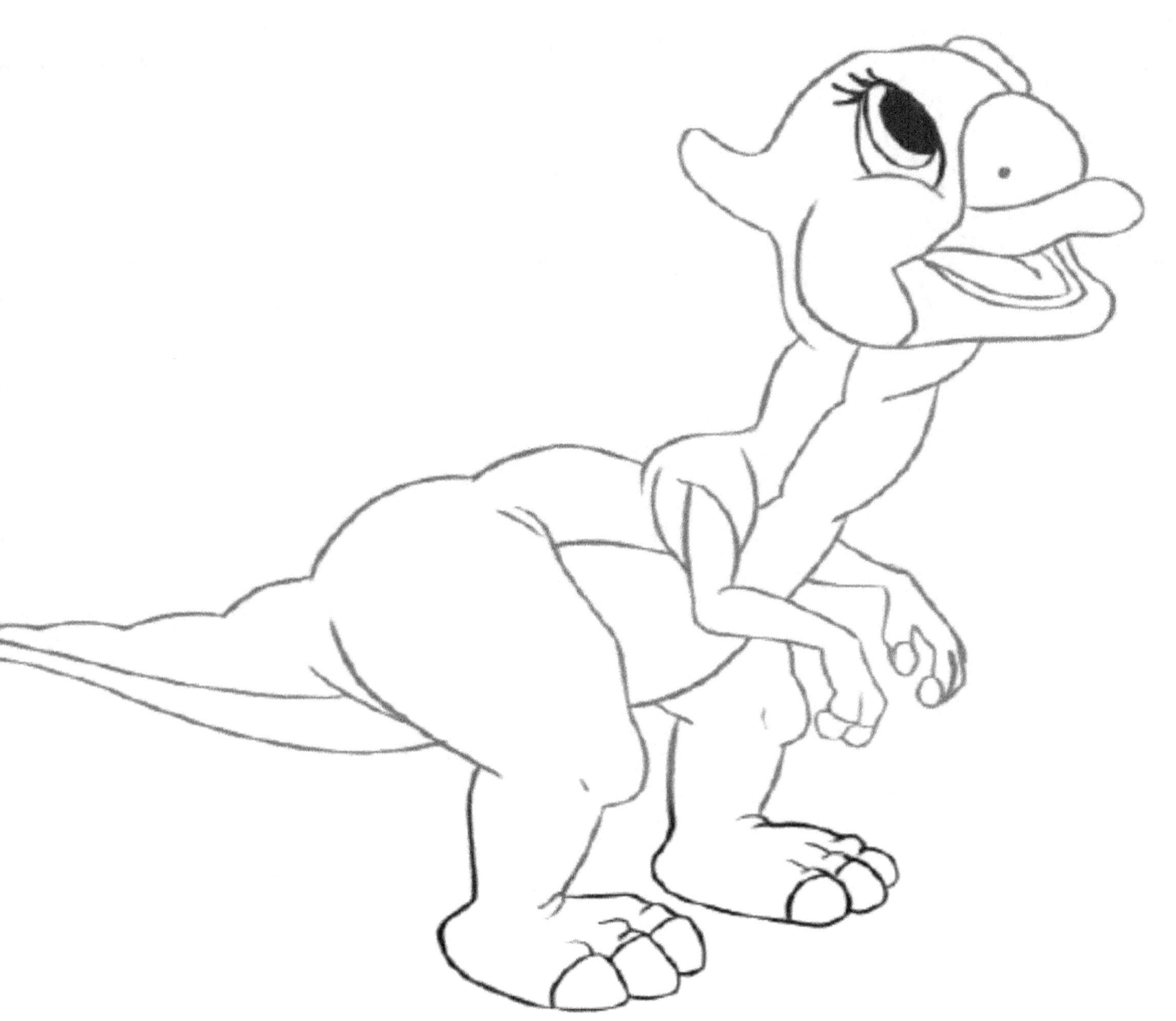

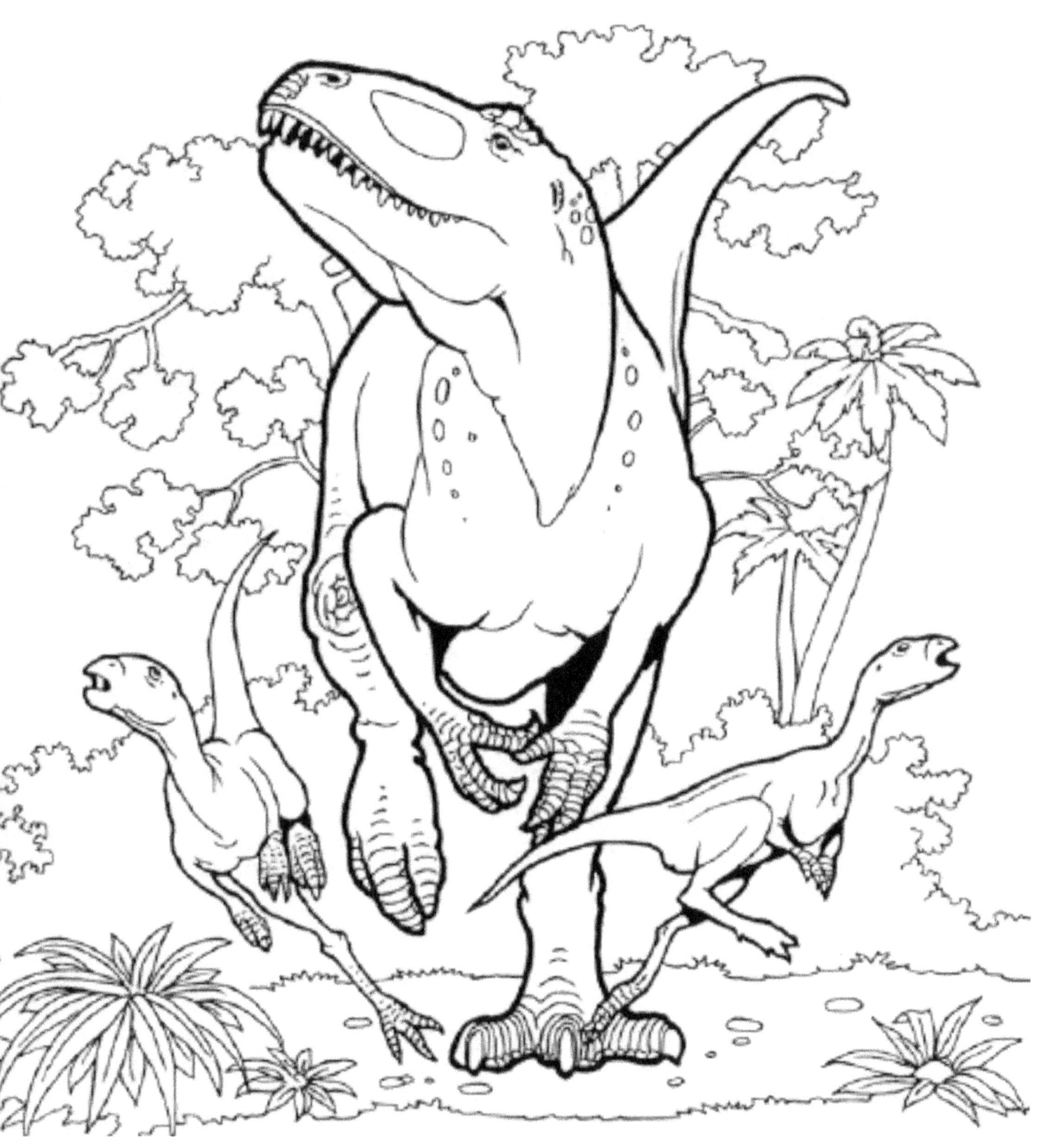

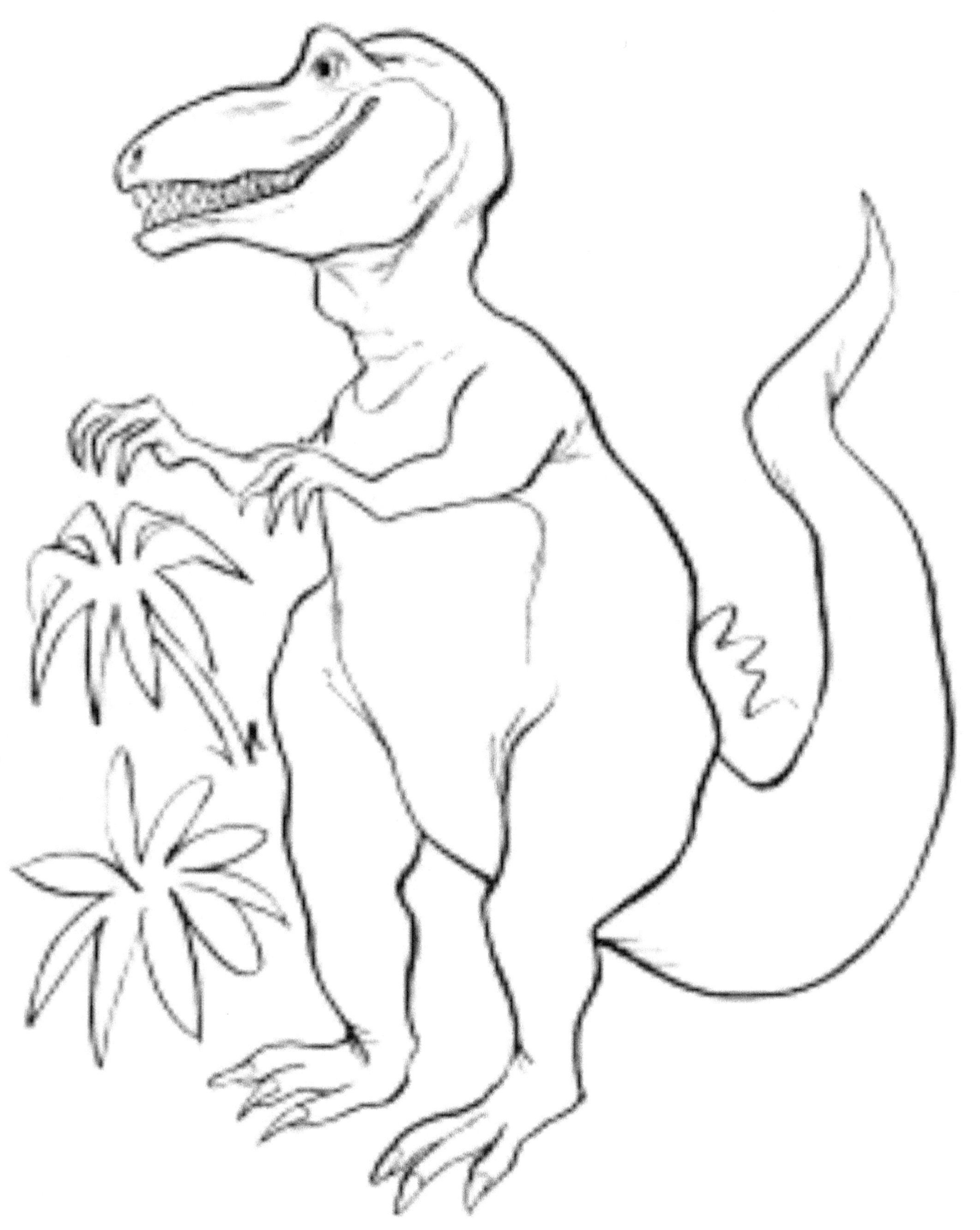

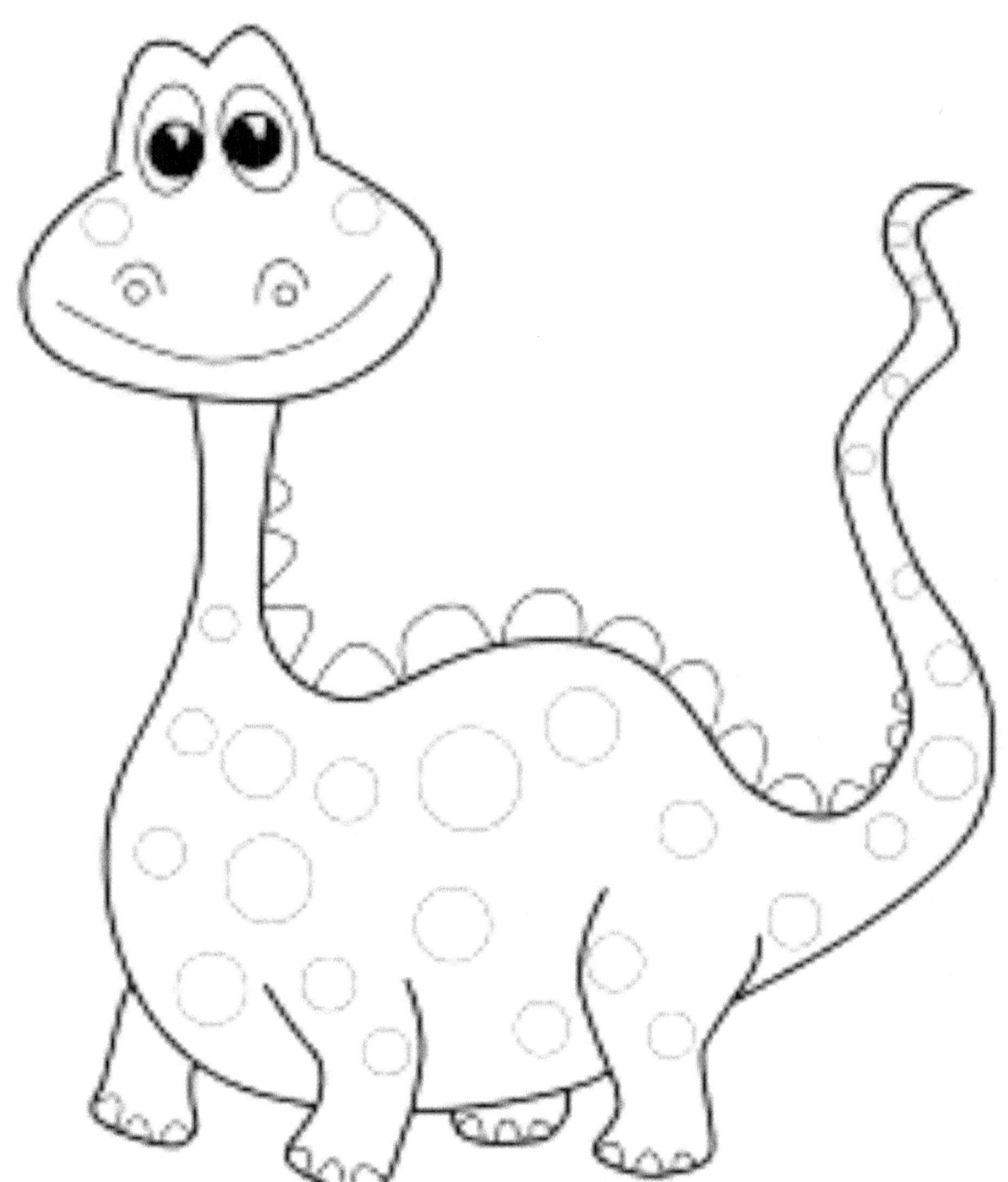

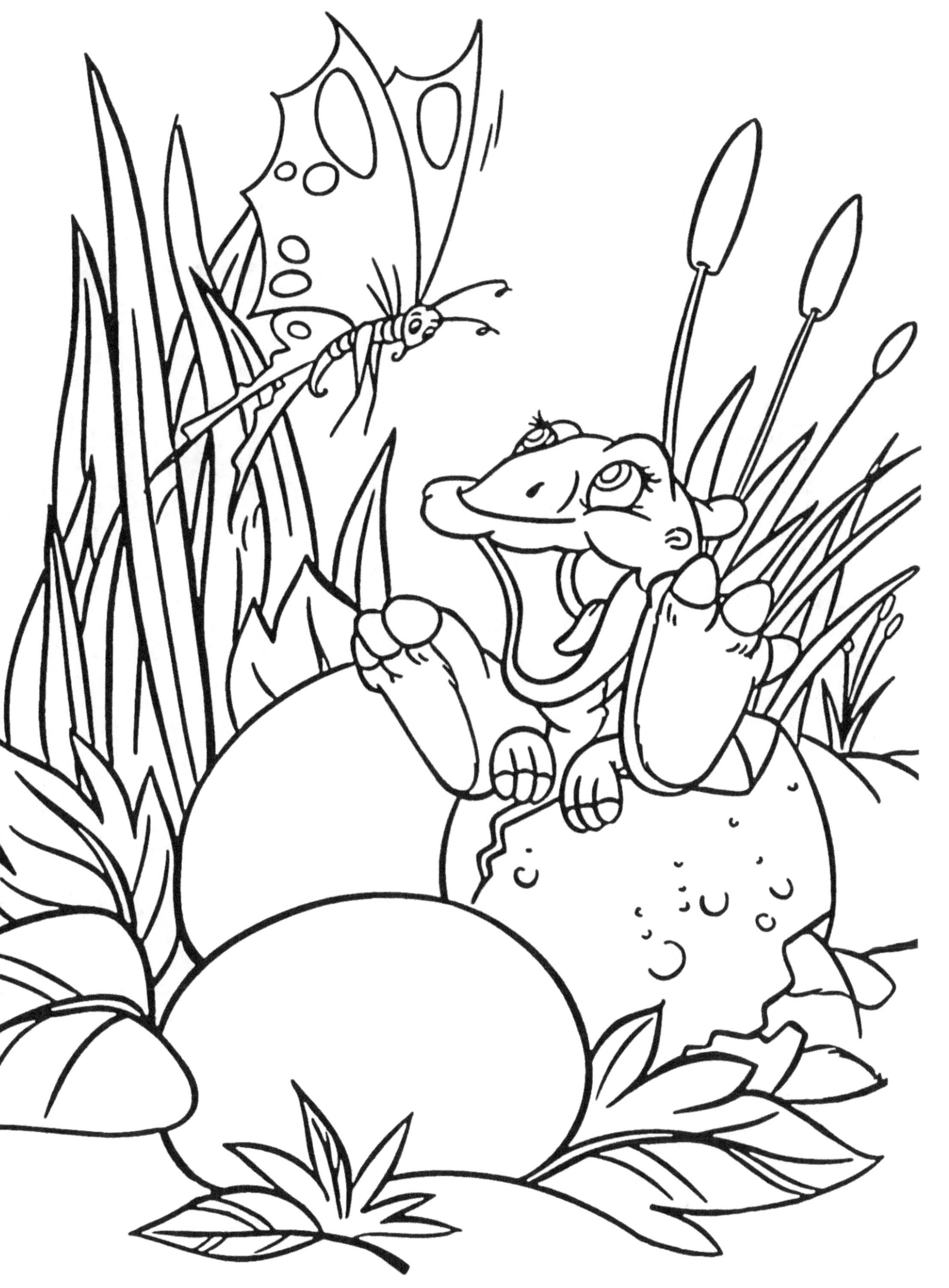

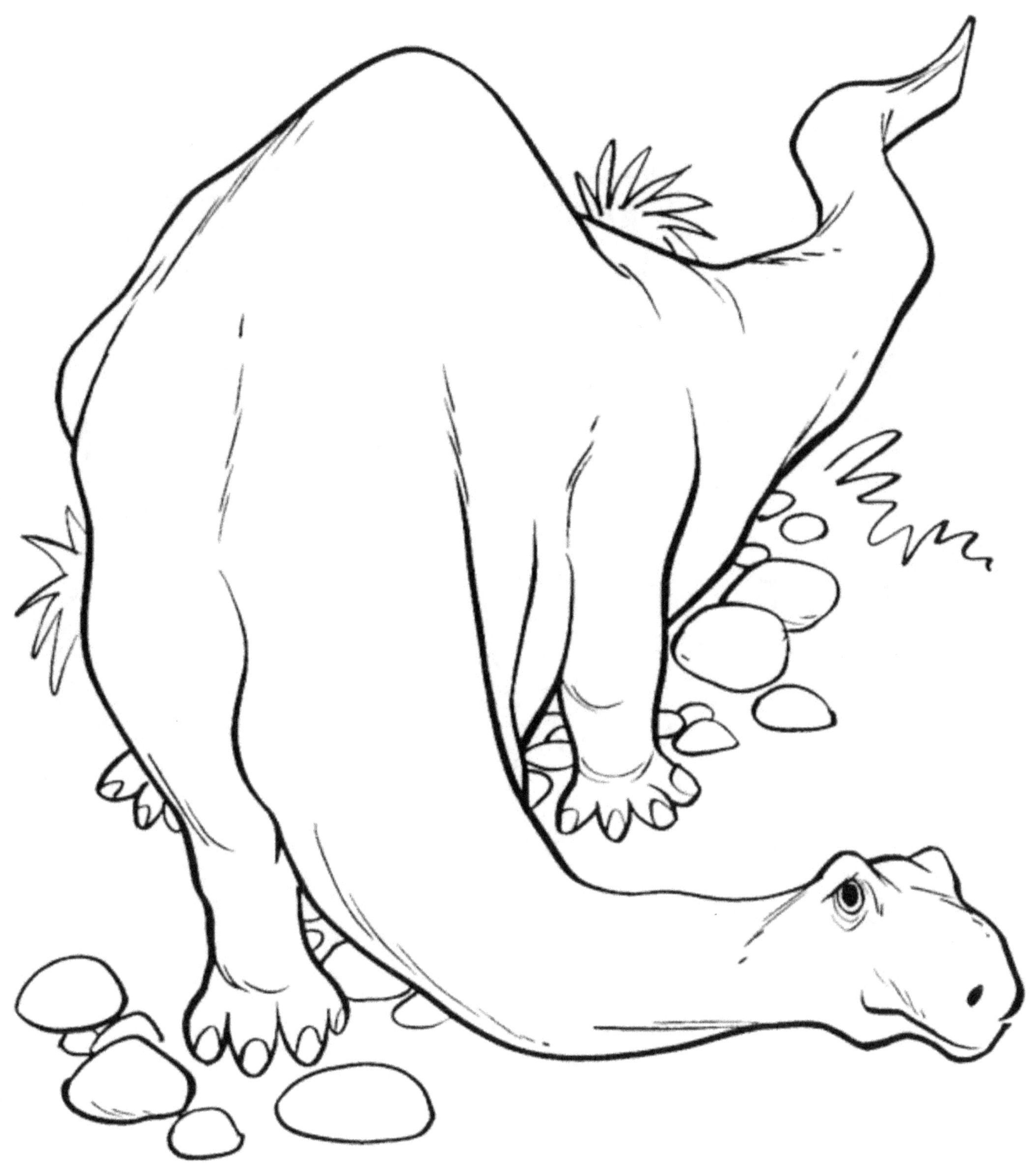